S N JOHNSON
BARRISTER AT LAW
BARTON MILL HOUSE
BARTON MILL ROAD
CANTERBURY 764899
DX 5342 CANTERBURY

W0013852

Rayden & Jackson's Law and Practice in Divorce and Family Matters

Volume 2   Statutory materials

Rayden & Jackson's Law and Practice in Divorce and Family Matters

Seventeenth edition

Volume 2   Statutory materials

The Honourable Mr Justice Wall
One of the Justices of Her Majesty's High Court of Justice

G J Maple LLB (LOND)
District Judge of the Principal Registry of the Family Division

Mark Everall MA (OXON)
One of Her Majesty's Counsel and of the Western Circuit

A K Biggs
Registrar of the Winchester District Probate Registry
Formerly of the Principal Registry of the Family Division

Consulting Editor

Dame Margaret Booth DBE
Formerly one of the Justices of Her Majesty's High Court of Justice

with specialist contributors

Butterworths
London, Edinburgh and Dublin
1997

United Kingdom	Butterworths a Division of Reed Elsevier (UK) Ltd, Halsbury House, 35 Chancery Lane, LONDON WC2A 1EL and 4 Hill Street, EDINBURGH EH2 3JZ
Australia	Butterworths, SYDNEY, ADELAIDE, BRISBANE, CANBERRA, MELBOURNE and PERTH
Canada	Butterworths Canada Ltd, TORONTO and VANCOUVER
Ireland	Butterworth (Ireland) Ltd, DUBLIN
Malaysia	Malayan Law Journal Sdn Bhd, KUALA LUMPUR
New Zealand	Butterworths of New Zealand Ltd, WELLINGTON and AUCKLAND
Singapore	Reed Elsevier (Singapore) Pte Ltd, SINGAPORE
South Africa	Butterworths Publishers (Pty) Ltd, DURBAN
USA	Michie, CHARLOTTESVILLE, Virginia

A CIP Catalogue record for this book is available from the British Library.

ISBN for the complete set of volumes 0 406 89040 4
ISBN for this volume 0 406 89431 0

Typeset by Columns Design Ltd, Reading, Berks.
Printed and bound in Great Britain by Clays Ltd, St Ives PLC

Contents

Volume 2   Statutory materials

Appendix 1   Chronological table of statutes

Appendix 1   Alphabetical table of statutes

Appendix 2 Chronological table of rules, regulations and orders

Appendix 2 Alphabetical table of rules, regulations and orders

Appendix 3   Court Fees

Statutes

Provisions repealed or prospectively repealed are printed in italics.

Statutes

Provisions repealed or prospectively repealed are printed in italics.

Note. The text follows the Acts as obtained from HM Printers. Chapter 1 (p 1) gives an account of the origin, background and jurisdiction of the courts in relation to matrimonial and family matters generally. It is sufficient here to point out that most of the provisions of the earlier Matrimonial Causes Acts were repealed and re-enacted by the Supreme Court of Judicature (Consolidation) Act 1952 (repealed finally by the Supreme Court Act 1981 (p 2767)) and sections of this Act in turn were substituted and considerably added to by the Matrimonial Causes Act 1937 (p 2088), which, as amended, was consolidated and replaced by the Matrimonial Causes Act 1950 (p 2120), itself amended and added to by later enactments, all of which were consolidated in the Matrimonial Causes Act 1965 (p 2221). New provisions relating to matrimonial causes were enacted by the Matrimonial Causes Act 1967 (p 2256). A major change in the law was effected by the Divorce Reform Act 1969 (p 2319)) and by the Matrimonial Proceedings and Property Act 1970 (p 2343), both of which came into force on 1 January 1971. The Act of 1969 and the bulk of the Act of 1970, together with most of the remaining unrepealed provisions of the Act of 1965 and the Nullity of Marriage Act 1971, were consolidated in the Matrimonial Causes Act 1973 (p 2468), which came into force on 1 January 1974. The main provisions relating to matrimonial causes are now to be found in the Act of 1973, as amended by subsequent legislation including the Matrimonial and Family Proceedings Act 1984. Nevertheless sections of the repealed Acts are retained for the purposes of reference and comparison. It is significant to trace how the law has been changed and to ascertain the 'mischief' to which such change is directed and the actual effect of such change. Statutes relating to marriage, status and relationships, including the Marriage Acts, the Legitimacy Acts, the Adoption Act 1976 and the Human Fertilisation and Embryology Act 1990, are also reproduced in whole or in part. The law relating to children has been radically altered by the Children Act 1989, so much so that it has been considered unnecessary to include such repealed statutes as the Guardianship Acts, the Affiliation Acts or the Children Act 1975, for all of which reference should be made to the 15th edition of this work. The Children Act 1989 is, however, printed in full. Statutes relevant to county court proceedings are reproduced in whole or in part, as are those which relate to matrimonial and other relevant proceedings in magistrates' courts. Those parts of the Courts and Legal Services Act 1990 which are relevant to this work are also reproduced. Appropriate cross-references are given.

Comparative Tables. For convenience, comparative tables are included for the following Acts, showing the relationship between them and the enactments consolidated in each case: Matrimonial Causes Act 1965 (p 2252); Matrimonial Causes Act 1973 (p 2535); Magistrates' Courts Act 1980 (p 2751); and Supreme Court Act 1981 (p 2816).

MATRIMONIAL CAUSES ACT 1857*

(20 & 21 Vict c 85)

An Act to amend the Law relating to divorce and matrimonial causes in England.

[*28 August 1857*]

WHEREAS *it is expedient to amend the law relating to divorce, and to constitute a Court with exclusive jurisdiction in matters matrimonial in England, and with authority in certain cases to decree the dissolution of a marriage: Be it therefore enacted, etc*

1.   (*Commencement of Act,* 1 *January* 1858.)
Note. Partly repealed by Statute Law Revision Act 1875 and wholly by Statute Law Revision Act 1892.

2. Jurisdiction in matters matrimonial now vested in Ecclesiastical Courts to cease. *As soon as this Act shall come into operation, all jurisdiction now exerciseable by any Ecclesiastical Court in England in respect of divorces à mensâ et thoro, suits of nullity of marriage, suits of jactitation of marriage, suits for restitution of conjugal rights, and in all causes, suits and matters matrimonial, shall cease to be so exerciseable, except so far as relates to the granting of marriage licences, which may be granted as if this Act had not been passed.*
Note. Repealed in part by Statute Law Revision Act 1892 and wholly by Supreme Court of Judicature (Consolidation) Act 1925, Sch 6. See now Supreme Court Act 1981, s 26 (p 2778).

3.   (*Power to enforce previous decrees and orders.*)
Note. Repealed by Statute Law Revision Act 1892.

4.   (*As to suits pending at commencement of Act.*)
Note. Repealed by Statute Law Revision Act 1875.

5.   (*Power to Judges whose jurisdiction is determined to deliver written judgments.*)
Note. Repealed by Statute Law Revision Act 1875.

6. Jurisdiction over causes matrimonial to be exercised by the Court for divorce and matrimonial causes. *As soon as this Act shall come into operation, all jurisdiction now vested in or exerciseable by any Ecclesiastical Court or person in England in respect of divorces à mensâ et thoro, suits of nullity of marriage, suits of restitution of conjugal rights, or jactitation of marriage, and in all causes, suits, and matters matrimonial, except in respect of marriage licences, shall belong to and be vested in Her Majesty, and such jurisdiction, together with the jurisdiction conferred by this Act, shall be exercised in the name of Her Majesty in a Court of Record to be called 'The Court for Divorce and Matrimonial Causes.'*
Note. Repealed in part by Statute Law Revision Act 1892, and wholly by Supreme Court of Judicature (Consolidation) Act 1925, Sch 6. See now Supreme Court Act 1981, ss 26, 61, Sch 1, para 3 (pp 2778, 2794, 2808).

7.   No decree for divorce à mensâ et thoro to be made hereafter, but a judicial separation. *No decree shall hereafter be made for a divorce à mensâ et thoro, but in all cases in which a decree for a divorce à mensâ et thoro might now be pronounced the Court may pronounce a decree for a judicial separation, which shall have the same force and the same consequence as a divorce à mensâ et thoro now has.*
Note. Repealed by Supreme Court of Judicature (Consolidation) Act 1925, Sch 6. See now Matrimonial Causes Act 1973, s 17 (p 2479), replacing Matrimonial Causes Act 1965, s 12

---

* This Act, most of which had already been repealed, was finally and totally repealed by Administration of Justice Act 1965, s 34(1) and Sch 2.

(p 2229), replacing Matrimonial Causes Act 1950, s 14(1), (2) (p 2125), replacing Act of 1925, s 185, as substituted by Matrimonial Causes Act 1937, s 5.

8. Judges of the Court. *The Lord Chancellor, the Lord Chief Justice of the Court of Queen's Bench, the Lord Chief Justice of the Court of Common Pleas, the Lord Chief Baron of the Court of Exchequer, the senior puisne judge for the time being in each of the three last-mentioned Courts, and the Judge of Her Majesty's Court of Probate constituted by any Act of the present session, shall be the Judges of the said Court.*

Note. Repealed by Statute Law Revision Act 1892.

9. Judge of the Court of Probate to be the Judge Ordinary, and shall have full authority, &c. *The Judge of the Court of Probate shall be called the Judge Ordinary of the said Court, and shall have full authority, either alone or with one or more of the other Judges of the said Court, to hear and determine all matters arising therein, except petitions for the dissolving of or annulling marriage, and applications for new trials of questions or issues before a jury, bills of exception, special verdicts, and special cases, and, except as aforesaid, may exercise all the powers and authority of the said Court.*

Note. Partly repealed by Statute Law Revision Act 1875 and wholly by Statute Law Revision Act 1892.

10. Petitions for dissolution of a marriage, &c., to be heard by three Judges. *All petitions, either for the dissolution or for a sentence of nullity of marriage, and applications for new trials of questions or issues before a jury, shall be heard and determined by three or more Judges of the said Court, of whom the Judge of the Court of Probate shall be one.*

Note. Repealed by Statute Law Revision Act 1875, and also by Statute Law Revision Act 1892. See also Matrimonial Causes Act 1858, s 18 (repealed) (p 2017); Matrimonial Causes Act 1860, ss 1, 2 (repealed) (p 2019).

11. (*Who to act as Judge, during absence of the Judge Ordinary.*)

Note. Repealed by Statute Law Revision Act 1892.

12. Sittings of the Court. *The Court for divorce and matrimonial causes shall hold its sittings at such place or places in London or Middlesex or elsewhere as Her Majesty in Council shall from time to time appoint.*

Note. Repealed by Supreme Court of Judicature (Consolidation) Act 1925, Sch 6.

13. Seal of the Court. *The Lord Chancellor shall direct a seal to be made for the said Court, and may direct the same to be broken, altered, and renewed, at his discretion; and all decrees and orders, or copies of decrees or orders, of the said Court, sealed with the said seal, shall be received in evidence.*

Note. Repealed by Supreme Court of Judicature (Consolidation) Act 1925, Sch 6. See now Supreme Court Act 1981, s 132 (p 2804).

14. (*Officers of the Court.*)

Note. Repealed by Judicature (Officers) Act 1879, s 29, which Act was repealed by Supreme Court of Judicature (Consolidation) Act 1925.

15. (*Power to Advocates, barristers, &c. of Ecclesiastical and Superior Courts to practise in the Court.*)

Note. Repealed by Statute Law Revision Act 1892.

16. Sentence of judicial separation may be obtained by husband or wife for adultery, &c. *A sentence of judicial separation (which shall have the effect of a divorce à mensâ et thoro under the existing law, and such other legal effect as herein mentioned), may* *be obtained, either by the husband or the wife, on the grounds of adultery, or cruelty, or desertion without cause for two years and upwards.*

Note. Repealed by Supreme Court of Judicature (Consolidation) Act 1925, Sch 6. See now Matrimonial Causes Act 1973, s 17 (p 2479), replacing Matrimonial Causes Act 1965, s 12 (p 2229), replacing Matrimonial Causes Act 1950, s 14(1) (p 2125), replacing Act of 1925, s 185(1) (p 2058), as substituted by Matrimonial Causes Act 1937, s 5.

17. Application for restitution of conjugal rights or judicial separation may be made by husband or wife by petition to Court &c. *Application for restitution of conjugal rights or for judicial separation on any one of the grounds aforesaid may be made by either husband or wife, by petition to the Court, or to any Judge of Assize of the Assizes held for the county in which the husband and wife reside or last resided together, and which Judge of Assize is hereby authorized and required to hear and determine such petition, according to the rules and regulations which shall be made under the authority of this Act; and the Court or Judge to which such petition is addressed, on being satisfied of the truth of the allegation therein contained, and that there is no legal ground why the same should not be granted, may decree such restitution of conjugal rights or judicial separation accordingly, and where the application is by the wife may make any order for alimony which shall be deemed just: Provided always, that any Judge of Assize to whom such petition shall be presented may refer the same to any of Her Majesty's Counsel or Serjeant-at-Law named in the Commission of Assize or nisi prius, and such counsel or serjeant shall, for the purpose of deciding upon the matters of such petition, have all the powers that any such Judge would have had by virtue of this Act or otherwise.*

Note. Partly repealed by Matrimonial Causes Act 1858, s 19, and by Statute Law Revision Act 1875. Wholly repealed by Supreme Court of Judicature (Consolidation) Act 1925, Sch 6. See Matrimonial Proceedings and Property Act 1970, s 20 (repealed) (p 2357) which abolished the right to claim restitution of conjugal rights, and Matrimonial Causes Act 1973, s 17 (p 2479), replacing Matrimonial Causes Act 1965, s 12 (p 2229); and ss 22–24, 26(1), 40 of the 1973 Act (pp 2482–2488, 2496, 2515), replacing Matrimonial Proceedings and Property Act 1970, ss 1–4, 24(1), 26 (pp 2345–2347, 2358, 2359), replacing Act of 1965, ss 13, 15, 16(3), 18(1), 19, 20(1), 30 and 34(6) (pp 2230, 2231, 2232, 2240, 2243), replacing Matrimonial Causes Act 1950, ss 14, 15, 19(4), 20(3), 27 and 29 (pp 2125, 2128, 2129, 2131, 2132), replacing Act of 1925, ss 185, 186 and 190(4) (pp 2058, 2059, 2061), and Matrimonial Causes Act 1937, s 10 (p 2091).

18. *(Powers of Judges of Assize for purposes of deciding applications under authority of this Act.)*

Note. This section introduced the system of appointment of what are now deputy High Court Judges: see Supreme Court Act 1981, s 9(4) (p 2773).

19. *(The Courts to regulate fees on proceedings before Judges, &c.)*

20. *(Orders may be reviewed.)*

Note. Sections 18, 19 and 20 repealed by Matrimonial Causes Act 1858, s 19; and also by Statute Law Revision Act 1875.

21. Wife deserted by her husband may apply to a police magistrate or justices in petty sessions for protection. *A wife deserted by her husband may at any time after such desertion, if resident within the metropolitan district, apply to a police magistrate, or if resident in the country to justices in petty sessions, or in either case to the Court, for an order to protect any money or property she may acquire by her own lawful industry, and property which she may become possessed of, after such desertion, against her husband or his creditors, or any person claiming under him: and such magistrate or justice or Court, if satisfied of the fact of such desertion, and that the same was without reasonable cause, and that the wife is maintaining herself by her own industry or property, may make and give to the wife an order protecting her earnings and property acquired since the commencement of such desertion, from her husband and all creditors and persons claiming under him, and such earnings and property shall belong to the wife as if she were a feme sole: Provided always, that every such order, if made by a police* *magistrate, or justices at petty sessions, shall, within ten days after the making thereof, be entered with the registrar of the County Court within whose jurisdiction the wife is resident; and that it shall be lawful for the husband, and any creditor or other person claiming under him, to apply to the Court, or to the magistrate or justices by whom such order was made, for the discharge thereof: Provided also, that if the husband or any creditor of or person claiming under the husband shall seize or continue to hold any property of the wife after notice of any such order, he shall be liable, at the suit of the wife (which she is hereby empowered to bring), to restore the specific property, and also for a sum equal to double the value of the property so seized or held after such notice as aforesaid: If any such order of protection be made, the wife shall during the continuance thereof be and be deemed to have been, during such desertion of her, in the like position in all respects, with regard to property and contracts, and suing and being sued, as she would be under this Act if she obtained a decree of judicial separation.*

Note. Partly repealed for all purposes and wholly repealed, so far as it related to the High Court, by Supreme Court of Judicature (Consolidation) Act 1925, Sch 6 and finally repealed by the Administration of Justice Act 1965, s 34 and Sch 2. This section was rendered obsolete by the Law Reform (Married Women and Tortfeasors) Act 1935 (p 2087), which enabled a married woman to acquire, hold, and dispose of property as if she were a single woman. See also Matrimonial Causes Act 1864, s 1 (repealed) (p 2021); Law Reform (Husband and Wife) Act 1962 (p 2215).

22. Court to act on principles of the Ecclesiastical Courts. *In all suits and proceedings, other than proceedings to dissolve any marriage, the said Court shall proceed and act and give relief on principles and rules which in the opinion of the said Court shall be as nearly as may be conformable to the principles and rules on which the Ecclesiastical Courts have heretofore acted and given relief, but subject to the provisions herein contained and to the rules and orders under this Act.*

Note. Repealed by Supreme Court of Judicature (Consolidation) Act 1925, Sch 6. See s 32 of that Act (p 2054) (repealed) replacing Supreme Court of Judicature Act 1873, s 23 (p 2027).

23. Decree of separation obtained during the absence of husband or wife may be reversed. *Any husband or wife, upon the application of whose wife or husband, as the case may be, a decree of judicial separation has been pronounced, may, at any time thereafter, present a petition to the Court praying for a reversal of such decree on the ground that it was obtained in his or her absence, and that there was reasonable ground for the alleged desertion, where desertion was the ground of such decree; and the Court may, on being satisfied of the truth of the allegations of such petition reverse the decree accordingly, but the reversal thereof shall not prejudice or affect the rights or remedies which any other person would have had in case such reversal had not been decreed, in respect of any debts, contracts, or acts of the wife incurred, entered into, or done between the times of the sentence of separation and of the reversal thereof.*

Note. Repealed by Supreme Court of Judicature (Consolidation) Act 1925, Sch 6. Cf Matrimonial Causes Act 1965, s 12(3) (p 2229) (repealed and not replaced), which replaced Matrimonial Causes Act 1950, s 14(3) (p 2125), which replaced Act of 1925, s 185 (p 2058), as amended by Matrimonial Causes Act 1937, s 5. The word 'and' in line 4 should be 'or'.

24. Court may direct payment of alimony to wife or to her trustee. *In all cases in which the Court shall make any decree or order for alimony, it may direct the same to be paid either to the wife herself or to any trustee on her behalf, to be approved by the Court, and may impose any terms or restrictions which to the Court may seem expedient, and may from time to time appoint a new trustee, if for any reason it shall appear to the Court expedient so to do.*

Note. Repealed by Supreme Court of Judicature (Consolidation) Act 1925, Sch 6. See Matrimonial Causes Act 1965, s 30(1) (p 2240), repealed, replacing Matrimonial Causes Act 1950, s 27(1) (p 2131), replacing Act of 1925, s 190(5) (p 2061).

25. In case of judicial separation the wife to be considered a feme sole with respect to property she may acquire, &c. *In every case of a judicial separation the wife shall, from the date of the sentence and whilst the separation shall continue, be considered as a* *feme sole with respect to property of every description which she may acquire or which may come to or devolve upon her; and such property may be disposed of by her in all respects as a feme sole, and on her decease the same shall, in case she shall die instestate, go as the same would have gone if her husband had been then dead: provided, that if any such wife should again cohabit with her husband, all such property as she may be entitled to when such cohabitation shall take place shall be held to her separate use, subject, however, to any agreement in writing made between herself and her husband whilst separate.*

Note. Repealed by Supreme Court of Judicature (Consolidation) Act 1925, Sch 6. See Matrimonial Causes Act 1973, s 18 (p 2480), replacing Matrimonial Proceedings and Property Act 1970, s 40 (p 2363), replacing Matrimonial Causes Act 1965, s 20(3) (p 2233), replacing Matrimonial Causes Act 1950, s 21 (p 2129), replacing Act of 1925, s 194 (p 2063), as amended by Law Reform (Married Women and Tortfeasors) Act 1935, s 5(1), Sch 1.

26. Also, for purposes of contract and suing. *In every case of a judicial separation the wife shall, whilst so separated, be considered as a feme sole for the purposes of contract, and wrongs and injuries, and suing and being sued in any civil proceeding; and her husband shall not be liable in respect of any engagement or contract she may have entered into, or for any wrongful act or omission by her, or for any costs she may incur as plaintiff or defendant; provided, that where upon any such judicial separation alimony has been decreed or ordered to be paid to the wife, and the same shall not be duly paid by the husband, he shall be liable for necessaries supplied for her use; provided also, that nothing shall prevent the wife from joining, at any time during such separation, in the exercise of any joint power given to herself and her husband.*

Note. Repealed by Supreme Court of Judicature (Consolidation) Act 1925, Sch 6. See Matrimonial Causes Act 1965, s 20(4) (p 2233), repealed, replacing Matrimonial Causes Act 1950, s 21 (p 2129), replacing Act of 1925, s 194 (p 2063), as amended by Law Reform (Married Women and Tortfeasors) Act 1935, s 5(1), Sch 1.

27. On adultery of wife or incest, &c., of husband, petition for dissolution of marriage may be presented. *It shall be lawful for any husband to present a petition to the said Court, praying that his marriage may be dissolved, on the ground that his wife has since the celebration thereof been guilty of adultery; and it shall be lawful for any wife to present a petition to the said Court, praying that her marriage may be dissolved, on the ground that since the celebration thereof her husband has been guilty of incestuous adultery, or of bigamy with adultery, or of rape, or of sodomy or bestiality, or of adultery coupled with such cruelty as without adultery would have entitled her to a divorce à mensâ et thoro, or of adultery coupled with desertion, without reasonable excuse, for two years or upwards; and every such petition shall state as distinctly as the nature of the case permits the facts on which the claim to have such marriage dissolved is founded: Provided that for the purposes of this Act incestuous adultery shall be taken to mean adultery committed by a husband with a woman with whom if his wife were dead he could not lawfully contract marriage by reason of her being within the prohibited degrees of consanguinity or affinity; and bigamy shall be taken to mean marriage of any person, being married, to any other person during the life of the former husband or wife, whether the second marriage shall have taken place within the dominions of Her Majesty or elsewhere.*

Note. Partly repealed by Matrimonial Causes Act 1923, s 2, Schedule. Wholly repealed by Supreme Court of Judicature (Consolidation) Act 1925, Sch 6. See now Matrimonial Causes Act 1973, s 1 (p 2471), replacing Divorce Reform Act 1969, ss 1, 2 (p 2319), replacing Matrimonial Causes Act 1965, s 1(1) (p 2223), replacing Matrimonial Causes Act 1950, s 1 (p 2150), replacing Act of 1925, s 176 (p 2054), as substituted by Matrimonial Causes Act 1937, s 2.

28. Adulterer to be a co-respondent. *Upon any such petition presented by a husband the petitioner shall make the alleged adulterer a co-respondent to the said petition, unless on special grounds, to be allowed by the Court, he shall be excused from so doing; and on every petition presented by a wife for dissolution of marriage the Court, if it see fit, may direct that the person with whom the husband is alleged to have committed adultery be made a respondent; and the parties or either of them may insist on having the contested matters of fact tried by a jury as herein-after mentioned.*

Note. Repealed by Supreme Court of Judicature (Consolidation) Act 1925, Sch 6. See now Matrimonial Causes Act 1973, s 49 (p 2522), replacing Matrimonial Causes Act 1965, s 4 (p 2225), replacing Matrimonial Causes Act 1950, s 4 (p 2122), replacing Act of 1925, ss 99(1)(h) and 177 (p 2055). See also Family Proceedings Rules 1991, r 2.32(1) (p 4608).

29. Court to be satisfied of absence of collusion. *Upon any such petition for the dissolution of a marriage, it shall be the duty of the Court to satisfy itself, so far as it reasonably can, not only as to the facts alleged, but also whether or not the petitioner has been in any manner accessory to or conniving at the adultery, or has condoned the same, and shall also inquire into any counter-charge which may be made against the petitioner.*

Note. Repealed by Supreme Court of Judicature (Consolidation) Act 1925, Sch 6. See now Matrimonial Causes Act 1973, s 1(3) (p 2471), replacing Divorce Reform Act 1969, s 2(2) (p 2320), replacing Matrimonial Causes Act 1965, s 5(1) (p 2225), replacing Matrimonial Causes Act 1950, s 4 (p 2122), replacing Act of 1925, s 178 (p 2055), as substituted by Matrimonial Causes Act 1937, s 4.

30. Dismissal of petition. *In case the Court, on the evidence in relation to any such petition, shall not be satisfied that the alleged adultery has been committed, or shall find that the petitioner has during the marriage been accessory to or conniving at the adultery of the other party to the marriage, or has condoned the adultery complained of, or that the petition is presented or prosecuted in collusion with either of the respondents, then and in any of the said cases the Court shall dismiss the said petition.*

Note. Repealed by Supreme Court of Judicature (Consolidation) Act 1925, Sch 6. See now Matrimonial Causes Act 1973, s 2(1) (p 2471), replacing Divorce Reform Act 1969, s 3(3) (p 2320), replacing Matrimonial Causes Act 1965, s 5(4) (p 2226), replacing Matrimonial Causes Act 1950, s 4 (p 2122), as amended by Matrimonial Causes Act 1963, s 4, replacing Supreme Court of Judicature (Consolidation) Act 1925, s 178 (p 2055), as substituted by Matrimonial Causes Act 1937, s 4.

31. Power of Court to pronounce decree for dissolving marriage. *In case the Court shall be satisfied on the evidence that the case of the petitioner has been proved, and shall not find that the petitioner has been in any manner accessory to or conniving at the adultery of the other party to the marriage, or has condoned the adultery complained of, or that the petition is presented or prosecuted in collusion with either of the respondents, then the Court shall pronounce a decree declaring such marriage to be dissolved: Provided always, that the Court shall not be bound to pronounce such decree if it shall find that the petitioner has during the marriage been guilty of adultery, or if the petitioner shall, in the opinion of the Court, have been guilty of unreasonable delay in presenting or prosecuting such petition, or of cruelty towards the other party to the marriage, or of having deserted or wilfully separated himself or herself from the other party before the adultery complained of, and without reasonable excuse, or of such wilful neglect or misconduct as has conduced to the adultery.*

Note. Repealed by Supreme Court of Judicature (Consolidation) Act 1925, Sch 6. See now Matrimonial Causes Act 1973, s 1(4) (p 2471), replacing Divorce Reform Act 1969, s 2(3) (p 2320), replacing Matrimonial Causes Act 1965, s 5(3), (4) (p 2226), replacing Matrimonial Causes Act 1950, s 4 (p 2122), as amended by Matrimonial Causes Act 1963, s 4, replacing the Act of 1925, s 178 (p 2055), as substituted by Matrimonial Causes Act 1937, s 4.

32. Alimony. *The Court may, if it shall think fit, on any such decree, order that the husband shall to the satisfaction of the Court secure to the wife such gross sum of money, or such annual sum of money for any term not exceeding her own life, as, having regard to her fortune (if any), to the ability of the husband, and to the conduct of the parties it shall deem reasonable, and for that purpose may refer it to any one of the conveyancing counsel of the Court of Chancery to settle and approve of a proper deed or instrument to be executed by all necessary parties; and the said Court may in such case, if it shall see fit, suspend the pronouncing of its decree until such deed shall have been duly executed; and upon any petition for dissolution of marriage the Court shall have the same power to make interim* *orders for payment of money, by way of alimony or otherwise, to the wife, as it would have in a suit instituted for judicial separation.*

Note. Repealed, with Matrimonial Causes Act 1866, s 1, by Matrimonial Causes Act 1907, s 2. See now Matrimonial Causes Act 1973, Part II (pp 2481 et seq), replacing Matrimonial Proceedings and Property Act 1970, Part I (pp 2345 et seq), which largely replaced Matrimonial Causes Act 1965, Parts II and III (pp 2230 et seq), replacing Matrimonial Causes Act 1950, ss 19–29 (pp 2128 et seq), replacing Supreme Court of Judicature (Consolidation) Act 1925, s 190 (p 2060), and Matrimonial Causes Act 1937, s 10 (p 2091).

33. Husband may claim damages from adulterers. *Any husband may, either in a petition for dissolution of marriage or for judicial separation, or in a petition limited to such object only, claim damages from any person on the ground of his having committed adultery with the wife of such petitioner, and such petition shall be served on the alleged adulterer and the wife, unless the Court shall dispense with such service, or direct some other service to be substituted; and the claim made by every such petition shall be heard and tried on the same principle, in the same manner, and subject to the same or the like rules and regulations as actions for criminal conversation are now tried and decided in Courts of Common Law; and all the enactments herein contained with reference to the hearing and decision of petitions to the Court shall, so far as may be necessary, be deemed applicable to the hearing and decision of petitions presented under this enactment; and the damages to be recovered on any such petition shall in all cases be ascertained by the verdict of a jury, although the respondents or either of them may not appear; and after the verdict has been given the Court shall have power to direct in what manner such damage shall be paid or applied, and to direct that the whole or any part thereof shall be settled for the benefit of the children (if any) of the marriage, or as a provision for the maintenance of the wife.*

Note. Repealed by Supreme Court of Judicature (Consolidation) Act 1925, Sch 6. See Law Reform (Miscellaneous Provisions) Act 1970, s 4 (p 2341) (which abolished the right to claim damages for adultery), replacing Matrimonial Causes Act 1965, s 41 (p 2247), replacing Matrimonial Causes Act 1950, s 30 (p 2132), replacing Act of 1925, s 189 (p 2060).

34. Power to Court to order adulterer to pay costs. *Whenever in any petition presented by a husband the alleged adulterer shall have been made a co-respondent, and the adultery shall have been established, it shall be lawful for the Court to order the adulterer to pay the whole or any part of the costs of the proceedings.*

Note. Repealed by Supreme Court of Judicature (Consolidation) Act 1925, Sch 6. See Law Reform (Miscellaneous Provisions) Act 1970, s 4 (p 2341).

35. Power to Court to make orders as to custody of children. *In any suit or other proceeding for obtaining a judicial separation or a decree of nullity of marriage, and on any petition for dissolving a marriage, the Court may from time to time, before making its final decree, make such interim orders, and may make such provision in the final decree, as it may deem just and proper with respect to the custody maintenance, and education of the children the marriage of whose parents is the subject of such suit or other proceeding, and may, if it shall think fit, direct proper proceedings to be taken for placing such children under the protection of the Court of Chancery.*

Note. Repealed by Supreme Court of Judicature (Consolidation) Act 1925, Sch 6. See now Matrimonial Causes Act 1973, s 42 and the notes thereto (p 2517), replacing Matrimonial Proceedings and Property Act 1970, s 18 (p 2356), replacing Matrimonial Causes Act 1965, ss 34(1), (4) and 46(2) (pp 2242, 2243, 2249), replacing Matrimonial Causes Act 1950, s 26 (p 2131), replacing Act of 1925, s 193 (p 2062), and Matrimonial Causes Act 1937, s 10 (p 2091).

36. Questions of fact may be tried before the Court. *In questions of fact arising in proceedings under this Act it shall be lawful for, but, except as herein-before provided, not obligatory upon, the Court to direct the truth thereof to be determined before itself, or before any one or more of the Judges of the said Court, by the verdict of a special or common jury.*

Note. Repealed by Administration of Justice Act 1925, s 29(4), Sch 5.

37. Where a question is ordered to be tried a jury may be summoned as in the Common Law Courts. *The Court, or any Judge thereof, may make all such rules and orders upon the sheriff or any other person for procuring the attendance of a special or common jury for the trial of such question as may now be made by any of the Superior Courts of Common Law at Westminster, and may also make any other orders which to such Court or Judge may seem requisite; and every such jury shall consist of persons possessing the like qualifications, and shall be struck, summoned, balloted for, and called in like manner, as if such jury were a jury for the trial of any cause in any of the said Superior Courts; and every juryman so summoned shall be entitled to the same rights, and subject to the same duties and liabilities, as if he had been duly summoned for the trial of any such cause in any of the said Superior Courts; and every party to any such proceeding shall be entitled to the same rights as to challenge and otherwise as if he were a party to any such cause.*

Note. Repealed by Administration of Justice Act 1925, s 27, Sch 4. (The *Rayden* editor of the time participated in one fully contested divorce trial, *Pearce v Pearce and McHugh* (October and November 1953, unreported), before a Judge and jury.)

38. Question to be reduced into writing, and a jury to be sworn to try it. Judge to have same powers as at nisi prius. *When any such question shall be so ordered to be tried such question shall be reduced into writing in such form as the Court shall direct, and at the trial the jury shall be sworn to try the said question, and a true verdict to give thereon according to the evidence; and upon every such trial the Court or Judge shall have the same powers, jurisdiction, and authority as any Judge of any of the said Superior Courts sitting at nisi prius.*

Note. Repealed by Administration of Justice Act 1925, s 27, Sch 4.

39. Bill of exceptions, special verdict, and special case. *Upon the trial of any such question or of any issue under this Act a bill of exceptions may be tendered, and a general or special verdict or verdicts, subject to a special case, may be returned, in like manner as in any cause tried in any of the said Superior Courts; and every such bill of exceptions, special verdict, and special case respectively shall be stated, settled, and sealed in like manner as in any cause tried in any of the said Superior Courts, and where the trial shall not have been had in the Court for Divorce and Matrimonial Causes shall be returned into such Court without any writ of error or other writ; and the matter of law in every such bill of exceptions, special verdict, and special cases shall be heard and determined by the full Court, subject to such rights of appeal as is hereinafter given in other cases.*

Note. Repealed by Matrimonial Causes Rules 1937, r 82(1).

40. Court may direct issues to try any fact. *It shall be lawful for the Court to direct one or more issue or issues to be tried in any Court of Common Law, and either before a Judge of Assize in any county or at the sittings for the trial of causes in London or Middlesex, and either by a special or common jury, in like manner as is now done by the Court of Chancery.*

Note. Repealed by Administration of Justice Act 1925, s 27, Sch 4; see Administration of Justice Act 1920, s 1, repealed and re-enacted by Supreme Court of Judicature (Consolidation) Act 1925, s 70(5), repealed by Courts Act 1971, s 56, Sch 11.

41. Affidavit in support of a petition. *Every person seeking a decree of nullity of marriage, or a decree of judicial separation, or a dissolution of marriage, or a decree in a suit of jactitation of marriage, shall, together with the petition or other application for the same, file an affidavit verifying the same so far as he or she is able to do so, and stating that there is not any collusion or connivance between the deponent and the other party to the marriage.*

Note. Repealed by Matrimonial Causes Rules 1937, r 82(1). As from 1 June 1966 the requirement as to affidavits in support of petitions was abolished: see SI 1966 No 560.

42. Service of petition. *Every such petition shall be served on the party to be affected thereby, either within or without Her Majesty's Dominions, in such manner as the Court shall by any general or special order from time to time direct, and for that purpose the Court shall have all the* *powers conferred by any statute on the Court of Chancery: Provided always, that the said Court may dispense with such service altogether in case it shall seem necessary or expedient so to do.*

Note. Repealed by Matrimonial Causes Rules 1950, r 82; see now Family Proceedings Rules 1991, r 2.9 (p 4608).

43. Examination of petitioner. *The Court may, if it shall think fit, order the attendance of the petitioner, and may examine him or her, or permit him or her to be examined or cross-examined on oath on the hearing of any petition, but no such petitioner shall be bound to answer any question tending to show that he or she has been guilty of adultery.*

Note. Repealed by Matrimonial Causes Rules 1937, r 82(1). See Matrimonial Causes Act 1859, s 6 (p 2019); Evidence Further Amendment Act 1869, s 3, repealed and re-enacted by the Supreme Court of Judicature (Consolidation) Act 1925, s 198 (p 2064), now replaced by Matrimonial Causes Act 1973, s 48(1) (p 2522), replacing Matrimonial Causes Act 1965, s 43(2) (p 2248), replacing Matrimonial Causes Act 1950, s 32(2) (p 2133). See also Matrimonial Causes Act 1973, s 48(2) (p 2522), replacing Matrimonial Causes Act 1965, s 43(3) (p 2249), replacing Act of 1950, s 32(4) (p 2133), replacing Supreme Court of Judicature (Consolidation) Act 1925, s 198A (p 2064), as inserted by Supreme Court of Judicature (Amendment) Act 1935, s 4.

44. Adjournment. *The Court may from time to time adjourn the hearing of any such petition, and may require further evidence thereon, if it shall see fit so to do.*

Note. Repealed by Statute Law Revision Act 1950, Sch 1.

45. Court may order settlement of property for benefit of innocent party and children of marriage. *In any case in which the Court shall pronounce a sentence of divorce or judicial separation for adultery of the wife, if it shall be made appear to the Court that the wife is entitled to any property either in possession or reversion, it shall be lawful for the Court, if it shall think proper, to order such settlement as it shall think reasonable to be made of such property or any part thereof, for the benefit of the innocent party, and of the children of the marriage, or either or any of them.*

Note. Repealed by Supreme Court of Judicature (Consolidation) Act 1925, Sch 6. See now Matrimonial Causes Act 1973, ss 24, 25 (pp 2488, 2489), replacing Matrimonial Proceedings and Property Act 1970, ss 4, 5 (pp 2346, 2347), replacing Matrimonial Causes Act 1965, ss 17(2) and 20(2) (pp 2232, 2233), replacing Matrimonial Causes Act 1950, s 24 (p 2130), replacing Matrimonial Causes Act 1937, s 10 (p 2091), which replaced Act of 1925, s 191 (p 2061).

46. Mode of taking evidence. *Subject to such rules and regulations as may be established as herein provided, the witnesses in all proceedings before the Court where their attendance can be had shall be sworn and examined orally in open Court: Provided that parties, except as hereinbefore provided, shall be at liberty to verify their respective cases in whole or in part by affidavit, but so that the deponent in every such affidavit shall, on the application of the opposite party or by direction of the Court, be subject to be cross-examined by or on behalf of the opposite party orally in open Court, and after such cross-examination may be re-examined orally in open Court as aforesaid by or on behalf of the party by whom such affidavit was filed.*

Note. Repealed by Matrimonial Causes Rules 1937, r 82(1). These Rules may be found in the 4th edition of this work. See now Supreme Court Act 1981, s 87(1) (p 2799).

47. Court may issue commissions or give orders for examination of witnesses abroad or unable to attend. *Provided, that where a witness is out of the jurisdiction of the Court, or where, by reason of his illness or from other circumstances, the Court shall not think fit to enforce the attendance of the witness in open Court, it shall be lawful for the Court to order a commission to issue for the examination of such witness on oath, upon interrogatories or otherwise, or if the witness be within the jurisdiction of the Court to order the examination of such witness on oath, upon interrogatories or otherwise, before any officer of the said Court, or other person to be named in such order for the purpose; and all the powers given to the Courts of Law at Westminster by the Acts of the Thirteenth Year of King George the Third, Chapter sixty-three (a), and of the First Year of King William the Fourth, Chapter Twenty-two (b), for* enabling the Courts of Law at Westminster to issue commissions and give orders for the examination of witnesses in actions depending in such Courts, and to enforce such examination, and all the provisions of the said Acts, and of any other Acts for enforcing or otherwise applicable to such examination and the witnesses examined, shall extend and be applicable to the Court and to the examination of witnesses under the commissions and orders of the said Court, and to the witnesses examined, as if such Court were one of the Courts of Law at Westminster, and the matter before it were an action pending in such Court.

Note. Repealed by Statute Law Revision Act 1892. See now Family Proceedings Rules 1991, r 2.28 (p 4608).

(a) Ie East India Company Act 1772 (repealed).

(b) Ie Evidence on Commission Act 1831 (repealed by Statute Law Revision Act 1963).

48. Rules of evidence in Common Law Courts to be observed. *The rules of evidence observed in the Superior Courts of Common Law at Westminster shall be applicable to and observed in the trial of all questions of fact in the Court.*

Note. Repealed by Statute Law Revision Act 1892.

49. Attendance of witnesses on the Court. *The Court may, under its seal, issue writs of subpœna or subpœna duces tecum, commanding the attendance of witnesses at such time and place as shall be therein expressed; and such writs may be served in any part of Great Britain or Ireland; and every person served with such writ shall be bound to attend, and to be sworn and give evidence in obedience thereto, in the same manner as if it had been a writ of subpœna or subpœna duces tecum issued from any of the said Superior Courts of Common Law in a cause pending therein, and served in Great Britain or Ireland, as the case may be: Provided that any petitioner required to be examined, or any person called as a witness or required or desiring to make an affidavit or deposition under or for the purposes of this Act, shall be permitted to make his solemn affirmation or declaration instead of being sworn in the circumstances and manner in which a person called as a witness or desiring to make an affidavit or deposition would be permitted so to do under the 'Common Law Procedure Act 1854,' in cases within the provisions of that Act.*

Note. The proviso was repealed by Statute Law Revision Act 1892; the remainder of the section by Statute Law Revision Act 1950, Sch 1. Common Law Procedure Act 1854, s 20, was repealed and replaced by Oaths Act 1888 (repealed). See now Oaths Act 1978 (p 2685).

50. Penalties for false evidence. *All persons wilfully deposing or affirming falsely in any proceeding before the Court shall be deemed to be guilty of perjury, and shall be liable to all the pains and penalties attached thereto.*

Note. Repealed by the Perjury Act 1911.

51. Costs. *The Court on the hearing of any suit, proceeding, or petition under this Act, and the House of Lords on the hearing of any appeal under this Act, may make such order as to costs as to such Court or House respectively may seem just: Provided always, that there shall be no appeal on the subject of costs only.*

Note. Repealed by Statute Law Revision Act 1892. See now Supreme Court Act 1981, s 51 (p 2790).

52. Enforcement of orders and decrees. *All decrees and orders to be made by the Court in any suit, proceeding, or petition to be instituted under authority of this Act shall be enforced and put in execution in the same or the like manner as the judgments, orders, and decrees of the High Court of Chancery may be now enforced and put in execution.*

Note. Repealed by Statute Law Revision Act 1892.

53. Power to make rules, &c., for procedure, and to alter them from time to time. *The Court shall make such rules and regulations concerning the practice and procedure* *under this Act as it may from time to time consider expedient, and shall have full power from time to time to revoke or alter the same.*

Note. Repealed by Administration of Justice Act 1925, s 29(4), Sch 5. See now Supreme Court Act 1981, s 84 (p 2798), and Matrimonial Causes Act 1973, s 50 (p 2523), replacing Matrimonial Causes Act 1967, s 7 (p 2359), and Family Proceedings Rules 1991 (p 4608).

54. Fees to be regulated. *The Court shall have full power to fix and regulate from time to time the fees payable upon all proceedings before it, all which fees shall be received, paid, and applied as herein directed: Provided always, that the said Court may make such rules and regulations as it may deem necessary and expedient for enabling persons to sue in the said Court in forma pauperis.*

Note. Partly repealed by Statute Law Revision Act 1892 and wholly, by Administration of Justice Act 1925, s 29(4), Sch 5. See now Supreme Court Act 1981, s 130 (p 2803).

55. Appeal from the Judge Ordinary to the full Court. *Either party dissatisfied with any decision of the Court in any matter which, according to the provisions aforesaid, may be made by the Judge Ordinary alone, may, within three calendar months after the pronouncing thereof, appeal therefrom to the full Court, whose decision shall be final.*

Note. Partly repealed by Statute Law Revision Act 1892; and, wholly, by Supreme Court of Judicature (Consolidation) Act 1925, Sch 6, which also repealed Supreme Court of Judicature Act 1881, s 9 ('Appeals under Divorce Act').

56. Appeal to the House of Lords in case of petition for dissolution of a marriage. *Either party dissatisfied with the decision of the full Court on any petition for the dissolution of a marriage may, within three months after the pronouncing thereof, appeal therefrom to the House of Lords if Parliament be then sitting, or if Parliament be not sitting at the end of such three months, then within fourteen days next after its meeting; and on the hearing of any such appeal the House of Lords may either dismiss the appeal or reverse the decree, or remit the case to the Court, to be dealt with in all respects as the House of Lords shall direct.*

Note. Repealed by Matrimonial Causes Act 1868, s 2; see also Matrimonial Causes Act 1858, s 17 (p 2017); Matrimonial Causes Act 1860, ss 2, 3 (pp 2019–2020); Supreme Court of Judicature Act 1881, s 9, and, now, Supreme Court Act 1981, s 16 (p 2775); Administration of Justice (Appeals) Act 1934, s 1 (p 2086), and Administration of Justice Act 1969, Part II (pp 2325 et seq).

57. Liberty to parties to marry again. *When the time hereby limited for appealing against any decree dissolving a marriage shall have expired, and no appeal shall have been presented against such decree, or when any such appeal shall have been dismissed, or when in the result of any appeal any marriage shall be declared to be dissolved, but not sooner, it shall be lawful for the respective parties thereto to marry again, as if the prior marriage had been dissolved by death: Provided always, that no clergyman in Holy Orders of the United Church of England and Ireland shall be compelled to solemnize the marriage of any person whose former marriage may have been dissolved on the grounds of his or her adultery, or shall be liable to any suit, penalty, or censure for solemnizing or refusing to solemnize the marriage of any such person.*

Note. Repealed by Supreme Court of Judicature (Consolidation) Act 1925, Sch 6. See now Matrimonial Causes Act 1965, s 8(2) (p 2228), replacing s 13(2) of the Matrimonial Causes Act 1950 (p 2125), replacing s 184 of the Act of 1925 (p 2058), as amended by s 12 of Matrimonial Causes Act 1937.

58. If minister of any Church, &c., refuses to perform marriage ceremony, any other minister may perform such service. *Provided always, that when any minister of any church or chapel of the United Church of England and Ireland shall refuse to perform such marriage service between any persons who but for such refusal would be entitled to have the same service performed in such church or chapel, such minister shall permit any other minister in*

Holy Orders of the said United Church, entitled to officiate within the diocese in which such church or chapel is situate, to perform such marriage service in such church or chapel.

Note. Repealed by Supreme Court of Judicature (Consolidation) Act 1925, Sch 6. See Matrimonial Causes Act 1965, s 8(2) (p 2228), replacing Matrimonial Causes Act 1950, s 13(2) (p 2125), replacing Act of 1925, s 184(2), (3) (p 2058), as substituted by Matrimonial Causes Act 1937, s 12 (no clergyman to be compelled to solemnise marriage of divorced person whose former spouse is living, or to permit marriage of such person in Church or Chapel of which he is minister).

59. No action in England for criminal conversation. *After this Act shall have come into operation no action shall be maintainable in England for criminal conversation.*

Note. Repealed by Statute Law Revision Act 1892.

60. (*All fees, except as herein provided, to be collected by stamps.*)

Note. Repealed by Statute Law Revision Act 1892.

61. (*Provisions concerning stamps for the Court of Probate to be applicable to the purposes of this Act.*)

Note. Repealed by Statute Law Revision Act 1892.

62. (*Expenses of the Court to be paid out of moneys to be provided by Parliament.*)

Note. Repealed by Supreme Court of Judicature (Officers) Act 1879.

63. (*Stamp duty on admission of Proctors, and annual certificates.*)

Note. Partly repealed by Statute Law Revision Act 1875; and, wholly, by Statute Law Revision Act 1892.

64. (*Compensation to Proctors: an annuity not exceeding half the annual loss sustained.*)

Note. Repealed by Statute Law Revision Act 1892.

65. (*Salary of Judge of Court of Probate, if appointed Judge of Court of Divorce, &c., £5,000.*)

Note. Partly repealed by Statute Law Revision Act 1875; and, wholly, by Statute Law Revision Act 1892.

66. Power to Secretary of State to order all letters patent, records &c., to be transmitted from all Ecclesiastical Courts. *Any one of Her Majesty's principal Secretaries of State may order every judge, registrar, or other officer of any Ecclesiastical Court in England or the Isle of Man, or any other person having the public custody of or control over any letters patent, records, deeds, processes, acts, proceedings, books, documents, or other instrument relating to marriages, or to suits for divorce, nullity of marriage, restitution of conjugal rights, or to any other matters or causes matrimonial, except marriage licences, to transmit the same, at such times and in such manner, to such places in London or Westminster, and under such regulations, as the said Secretary of State may appoint; and if any judge, registrar, officer, or other person shall wilfully disobey such order he shall for the first offence forfeit the sum of one hundred pounds, to be recoverable by any registrar of the Court of Probate as a debt under this Act in any of the Superior Courts at Westminster, and for the second and subsequent offences the Judge Ordinary may commit the person so offending to prison for any period not exceeding three calendar months, provided that the warrant of committal be countersigned by one of Her Majesty's principal Secretaries of State, and the said persons so offending shall forfeit all claim to compensation under this Act.*

Note. Repealed by Supreme Court of Judicature (Consolidation) Act 1925, Sch 6 and re-enacted by s 199 of that Act (p 2065) subsequently repealed by Public Records Act 1958.

67. Rules, &c., to be laid before Parliament. *All rules and regulations concerning practice or procedure, or fixing or regulating fees, which may be made by the Court under this Act, shall be laid before both Houses of Parliament within one month after the making thereof, if Parliament be then sitting, or if Parliament be not then sitting, within one month after the commencement of the then next session of Parliament.*

Note. Partly repealed by Statute Law Revision Act 1892; and wholly, by Administration of Justice Act 1925, s 29(4), Sch 5. See now Supreme Court Act 1981, s 84 (p 2798) and Matrimonial Causes Act 1973, s 50 (p 2523).

68. (*Yearly account of fees, &c., to be laid before Parliament.*)
Note. Repealed by Supreme Court of Judicature (Officers) Act 1879, s 29 as amended by Statute Law Revision Act 1894.

MATRIMONIAL CAUSES ACT 1858

(21 & 22 Vict c 108)

An Act to amend the Act of the Twentieth and Twenty-first Victoria Chapter Eighty-five. *
[*2 August 1858*]

WHEREAS in the last session of Parliament an Act was passed, intituled an Act to amend the law relating to divorce and matrimonial causes in England, and whereas it is expedient to amend the same: Be it therefore enacted, etc.
Note. Preamble repealed by Statute Law Revision Act 1892.

1. The Judge Ordinary of the Court for Divorce and Matrimonial Causes may sit in Chambers. *It shall be lawful for the Judge Ordinary of the Court for Divorce and Matrimonial Causes for the time being to sit in Chambers for the despatch of such part of the business of the said Court as can in the opinion of the said Judge Ordinary, with advantage to the suitors, be heard in Chambers; and such sittings shall from time to time be appointed by the said Judge Ordinary.*
Note. Repealed by Statute Law Revision Act 1892.

2. (*The Treasury to cause Chambers to be provided.*)
Note. Partly repealed by Statute Law Revision Act 1875; and wholly, by Statute Law Revision Act 1892.

3. Powers of Judge when sitting in Chambers. *The said Judge Ordinary when so sitting in Chambers shall have and exercise the same power and jurisdiction in respect of the business to be brought before him as if sitting in open Court.*
Note. Repealed by Statute Law Revision Act 1892.

4. The registrars to do all acts heretofore done by surrogates. *The registrars of the principal registry of the Court of Probate shall be invested with and shall and may exercise with reference to proceedings in the Court of Divorce and Matrimonial Causes the same power and authority which surrogates of the Official Principal of the Court of Arches could or might before the passing of the twentieth and twenty-first Victoria, chapter seventy-seven† have exercised in chambers with reference to proceedings in that Court.*
Note. Repealed by Supreme Court of Judicature (Consolidation) Act 1925, Sch 6.

---

* Ie Matrimonial Causes Act 1857 (p 2002).
† Ie Court of Probate Act 1857.

5. Evidence on which divorce obtained prior to 20 & 21 Vict c 85,* may be used in support of petition in the Court for Divorce and Matrimonial Causes. *In every cause in which a sentence of divorce and separation from bed, board, and mutual cohabitation has been given by a competent Ecclesiastical Court before the Act of the twentieth and twenty-first Victoria, chapter eighty-five,* came into operation, the evidence in the cause in which such sentence was pronounced in such Ecclesiastical Court may, whenever from the death of a witness or from any other cause it may appear to the Court reasonable and proper, be received on the hearing of any petition which may be presented to the said Court for Divorce and Matrimonial Causes.*

Note. Repealed by Administration of Justice Act 1925, s 27, Sch 4.

6. Wives deserted by their husbands may apply to the judge for an order to protected property, &c., acquired by them. *Every wife deserted by her husband, wheresoever resident in England, may, at any time after such desertion, apply to the said Judge Ordinary for an order to protect any money or property in England she may have acquired or may acquire by her own lawful industry, and any property she may have become possessed of or may become possessed of after such desertion against her husband and his creditors, and any person claiming under him; and the Judge Ordinary shall exercise in respect of every such application all the powers conferred upon the Court for Divorce and Matrimonial Causes under the twentieth and twenty-first Victoria, chapter eighty-five,* section twenty-one.*

Note. Repealed by Supreme Court of Judicature (Consolidation) Act 1925, Sch 6, and not re-enacted. See Matrimonial Causes Act 1857, s 21, and note thereto (p 2004).

7. Provisions respecting property of wife to extend to property vested in her as executrix, &c. *The provisions contained in this Act and in the said Act of the twentieth and twenty-first Victoria, chapter eighty-five,* respecting the property of a wife who has obtained a decree for judicial separation or an order for protection, shall be deemed to extend to property to which such wife has become or shall become entitled as executrix, administratrix, or trustee since the sentence of separation or the commencement of the desertion (as the case may be); and the death of the testator or intestate shall be deemed to be the time when such wife became entitled as executrix or administratrix.*

Note. Repealed by Supreme Court of Judicature (Consolidation) Act 1925, Sch 6. See now Matrimonial Causes Act 1973, ss 24, 25 (pp 2488, 2489), replacing Matrimonial Proceedings and Property Act 1970, ss 4, 5 (pp 2346, 2347), replacing (with saving for sub-s (3) thereof) Matrimonial Causes Act 1965, s 20 (p 2232), replacing Matrimonial Causes Act 1950, s 21 (p 2129), replacing s 194 of the Act of 1925 (p 2063), and Law Reform (Married Women and Tortfeasors) Act 1935, s 5(1) and Sch 1.

8. Order for protection of earnings, &c., of wife to be deemed valid. *In every case in which a wife shall under this Act or under the said Act of the twentieth and twenty-first Victoria, chapter eighty-five,* have obtained an order to protect her earnings or property, or a decree for judicial separation, such order or decree shall, until reversed or discharged, so far as necessary for the protection of any person or corporation who shall deal with the wife, be deemed valid and effectual; and no discharge, variation, or reversal of such order or decree shall prejudice or affect any rights or remedies which any person would have had in case the same had not been so reversed, varied, or discharged in respect of any debts, contracts, or acts of the wife incurred, entered into, or done between the times of the making such order or decree and the discharge, variation, or reversal thereof; and property of or to which the wife is possessed or entitled for an estate in remainder or reversion at the date of the desertion or decree (as the case may be), shall be deemed to be included in the protection given by the order or decree.*

Note. Repealed by Supreme Court of Judicature (Consolidation) Act 1925, Sch 6. See now Matrimonial Causes Act 1973, ss 24, 25 (pp 2488, 2489), replacing Matrimonial Proceedings and Property Act 1970, ss 4, 5 (pp 2346, 2347), replacing (with saving for sub-s (3) thereof) Matrimonial Causes Act 1965, s 20 (p 2232), replacing Matrimonial Causes Act 1950, s 21

---

* Ie Matrimonial Causes Act 1857 (p 2002).

(p 2129), replacing s 194 of the Act of 1925 (p 2063), and see note to s 7 above. See also Act of 1925, s 195 (p 2064). This section was repealed by the Act of 1950, Schedule, and not re-enacted.

9. Order to state the time at which the desertion commenced. *Every order which shall be obtained by a wife under the said Act of the twentieth and twenty-first Victoria, chapter eighty-five,* * or under this Act, for the protection of her earnings or property, shall state the time at which the desertion in consequence whereof the order is made commenced; and the order shall, as regards all persons dealing with such wife in reliance thereon, be conclusive as to the time when such desertion commenced.*

Note. Repealed by Supreme Court of Judicature (Consolidation) Act 1925, Sch 6, and not re-enacted.

10. Indemnity to corporations, &c., making payments under orders afterwards reversed. *All persons and corporations who shall, in reliance on any such order or decree as aforesaid, make any payment to, or permit any transfer or act to be made or done by, the wife who has obtained the same, shall, notwithstanding such order or decree may then have been discharged, reversed, or varied, or the separation of the wife from her husband may have ceased, or at some time since the making of the order or decree been discontinued, be protected and indemnified in the same way in all respects as if, at the time of such payment, transfer, or other act, such order or decree were valid and still subsisting without variation in full force and effect, and the separation of the wife from her husband had not ceased or been discontinued, unless at the time of such payment, transfer, or other act such persons or corporations had notice of the discharge, reversal, or variation of such order or decree, or of the cessation or discontinuance of such separation.*

Note. Repealed by Supreme Court of Judicature (Consolidation) Act 1925, Sch 6. See now Matrimonial Causes Act 1973, ss 24, 25 (pp 2488, 2489), replacing Matrimonial Proceedings and Property Act 1970, ss 4, 5 (pp 2346, 2347), replacing (with saving for sub-s (3) thereof) Matrimonial Causes Act 1965, s 20 (p 2232), replacing Matrimonial Causes Act 1950, s 21 (p 2129). See also s 195 of the Act of 1925 (p 2064): this section was repealed by the Act of 1950, Schedule, and not re-enacted.

11. Where alleged adulterer a co-respondent Court may order him to be dismissed from the suit. *In all cases now pending, or hereafter to be commenced in which, on the petition of a husband for a divorce, the alleged adulterer is made a co-respondent, or in which, on the petition of a wife, the person with whom the husband is alleged to have committed adultery is made a respondent, it shall be lawful for the Court, after the close of the evidence on the part of the petitioner, to direct such co-respondent or respondent to be dismissed from the suit, if it shall think there is not sufficient evidence against him or her.*

Note. Repealed by Supreme Court of Judicature (Consolidation) Act 1925, Sch 6. See now Matrimonial Causes Act 1973, s 49(3) (p 2522), replacing Matrimonial Causes Act 1965, s 4(3) (p 2225), replacing Matrimonial Causes Act 1950, s 5 (p 2122), replacing Act of 1925, s 179 (p 2056).

12. (*Persons who administer oaths under 20 & 21 Vict c 77,† to administer under 20 & 21 Vict c 85.* *)

Note. Repealed by Statute Law Revision Act 1892.

13. Bills of proctors, attorneys, &c., to be subject to taxation. *The bill of any proctor, attorney, or solicitor, for any fees, charges, or disbursements in respect of any business transacted in the Court for Divorce and Matrimonial Causes, and whether the same was transacted before the full Court or before the Judge Ordinary, shall, as well between proctor or attorney or solicitor and client, as between party and party, be subject to taxation by any one of the registrars belonging to the principal registry of the Court of Probate, and the mode in*

---

† Court of Probate Act 1857.

* Matrimonial Causes Act 1857 (p 2002).

which any such bill shall be referred for taxation, and by whom the costs of taxation shall be paid, shall be regulated by the rules and orders to be made under the Act of the twentieth and twenty-first of Victoria, chapter eighty-five,* and the certificate of the registrar of the amount at which such bill is taxed shall be subject to appeal to the Judge of the said Court.

Note. Repealed by Statute Law Revision Act 1892.

14. Power to enforce decree as to costs. *The Judge Ordinary of the Court for Divorce and Matrimonial Causes, and the registrars of the principal registry of the Court of Probate, shall respectively, in any case where an Ecclesiastical Court having matrimonial jurisdiction had, previously to the commencement of the Act of the twentieth and twenty-first Victoria, chapter eighty-five,* made any order or decree in respect of costs, have the same power of taxing such costs, and enforcing payment thereof, or of otherwise carrying such order or decree into effect, as if the cause wherein such decree was made had been originally commenced and prosecuted in the said Court for Divorce and Matrimonial Causes: provided that in taxing any such costs, or any other costs incurred in causes depending in any Ecclesiastical Court previously to the commencement of the said recited Act, all fees, charges, and expenses shall be allowed which might have been legally made, charged, and enforced according to the practice of the Court of Arches.*

Note. Repealed by Administration of Justice Act 1925, s 27, Sch 4.

15. Judge to exercise power and authority over proctors, &c. *The Judge Ordinary of the Court for Divorce and Matrimonial Causes shall have and exercise, over proctors, solicitors, and attorneys practising in the said Court, the like authority and control as is now exercised by the judges of any Court of equity or of common law over persons practising therein as proctors, solicitors, or attorneys.*

Note. Repealed by Supreme Court of Judicature (Consolidation) Act 1925, Sch 6.

16. (*Commissioners may be appointed in the Isle of Man, &c.*)

Note. Repealed by Statute Law Revision Act 1892.

17. Appeal in cases of nullity of marriage to lie to the House of Lords. *Whereas doubts may be entertained whether the rights of appeal given by the Act of the twentieth and twenty-first Victoria, chapter eighty-five,* section fifty-six, extends to sentences on petitions for nullity of marriage: be it enacted and declared, that either party dissatisfied with any such sentence may appeal therefrom in the same manner, within the same time, and subject to the same regulations as affect appeals against sentences on petitions for the dissolution of marriage.*

Note. Repealed by Matrimonial Causes Act 1868, s 2. For Matrimonial Causes Act 1857, s 56, see p 2012.

18. Judge Ordinary may grant rule nisi for new trial, &c. *Where any trial shall have been heard by a jury before the full Court or before the Judge Ordinary, or upon any issue directed by the full Court or by the Judge Ordinary, it shall be lawful for the Judge Ordinary, subject to any rules to be hereafter made, to grant a rule nisi for a new trial, but no such rule shall be made absolute except by the full Court.*

Note. Partly repealed by Statute Law Revision Act 1875; and, wholly, by Statute Law Revision Act 1892.

19. So much of 20 & 21 Vict c 85* as to be applications to judges of assizes repealed. *So much of the Act of the twentieth and twenty-first Victoria, chapter eighty-five,* as authorises application to be made for restitution of conjugal rights or for judicial separation by petition to any judge of assize, and as relates to the proceedings on such petition, shall be and the same is hereby repealed.*

---

* Matrimonial Causes Act 1857 (p 2002).

Note. Repealed by Statute Law Revision Act 1875.

20.   (*Affidavits, before whom to be sworn when parties making them reside in foreign parts.*)

21.   (*Affidavits, before whom to be sworn.*)

22.   (*Persons forging seal or signature guilty of felony.*)

23.   (*Persons taking a false oath before a surrogate guilty of perjury.*)
Note.   The above four sections were repealed by Commissioners for Oaths Act 1889, s 12.

MATRIMONIAL CAUSES ACT 1859†

(22 & 23 Vict c 61)

An Act to make further provision concerning the Court for Divorce and Matrimonial Causes.
[*13 August 1859*]
† The whole Act was repealed by Supreme Court of Judicature (Consolidation) Act 1925, Sch 6.

1.   (*Judges of the Queen's Bench, &c., to be judges of the Court for Divorce.*)
Note.   Repealed by Statute Law Revision Act 1892.

2.   (*Judge Ordinary and eight of the other judges to appoint the sittings of the full Court.*)
Note.   Repealed by Matrimonial Causes Act 1860, s 4, and also by Statute Law Revision Act 1892.

3.   (*Precedence of the Judge Ordinary.*)
Note.   Repealed by Statute Law Revision Act 1892.

4. The Court may make orders as to custody of children after a final decree of separation. *The Court after a final decree of judicial separation, nullity of marriage, or dissolution of marriage, may upon application (by petition) for this purpose make, from time to time, all such orders and provision with respect to the custody, maintenance, and education of the children the marriage of whose parents was the subject of the decree, or for placing such children under the protection of the Court of Chancery, as might have been made by such final decree or by interim orders in case the proceedings for obtaining such decree were still pending; and all orders under this enactment may be made by the Judge Ordinary alone or with one or more of the other judges of the Court.*
Note.   Partly repealed by Statute Law Revision Act 1875; and, wholly, by Supreme Court of Judicature (Consolidation) Act 1925, Sch 6. See now Matrimonial Causes Act 1973, ss 42, 52(1) (pp 2517, 2525), replacing Matrimonial Proceedings and Property Act 1970, ss 18, 19, 27(1) (pp 2356, 2359), replacing Matrimonial Causes Act 1965, ss 34(1), (4), 46(2) (pp 2242, 2243, 2249), replacing Matrimonial Causes Act 1950, s 26 (p 2131), replacing Act of 1925, s 193 (p 2062), as extended by Matrimonial Causes Act 1937, s 10(4) (p 2092).

5. As to marriage settlements of parties after final decrees of nullity of marriage. *The Court after a final decree of nullity of marriage or dissolution of marriage may inquire into the existence of ante-nuptial or post-nuptial settlements made on the parties whose marriage is the subject of the decree, and may make such orders with reference to the application of the whole or a portion of the property settled either for the benefit of the children of the marriage, or of their respective parents as to the Court shall seem fit.*
Note.   Extended by Matrimonial Causes Act 1878, s 3; and repealed by Supreme Court of Judicature (Consolidation) Act 1925, Sch 6 (p 2065). See now Matrimonial Causes Act 1973,

ss 24, 25, 52(1) (pp 2488, 2489, 2525), replacing Matrimonial Proceedings and Property Act 1970, ss 4, 5, 27(1) (pp 2346, 2347, 2359), replacing Matrimonial Causes Act 1965, ss 17(1), 19, 46(2) (pp 2231, 2232, 2249), replacing Matrimonial Causes Act 1950, s 25 (p 2131), replacing Act of 1925, s 192 (p 2062).

6. On a petition by wife on account of adultery, &c., both husband and wife competent, &c., to give evidence. *On any petition presented by a wife, praying that her marriage may be dissolved by reason of her husband having been guilty of adultery coupled with cruelty, or of adultery coupled with desertion, the husband and wife respectively shall be competent and compellable to give evidence of or relating to such cruelty or desertion.*

Note. Repealed by Supreme Court of Judicature (Consolidation) Act 1925, Sch 6. See now Matrimonial Causes Act 1973, s 48 (p 2522), replacing Matrimonial Causes Act 1965, s 43 (p 2248), replacing Matrimonial Causes Act 1950, s 32 (p 2133), replacing Act of 1925, s 198 (p 2064), which repealed and re-enacted Evidence Further Amendment Act 1869, s 3, and which was extended by Supreme Court of Judicature (Amendment) Act 1935, s 4 (p 2086).

7. Extension of right of appeal to House of Lords. *The right of appeal to the House of Lords given by the fifty-sixth section of the recited Act, shall extend to all sentences and final judgments on petitions under the Legitimacy Declaration Act 1858.*

Note. Repealed by Statute Law Revision Act 1892 and by Supreme Court of Judicature (Consolidation) Act 1925, Sch 6: see Administration of Justice (Appeals) Act 1934, s 1 (p 2086). For 'recited Act' (ie Matrimonial Causes Act 1857), s 56, see p 2012.

MATRIMONIAL CAUSES ACT 1860*

(23 & 24 Vict c 144)

An Act to amend the procedure and powers of the Court for Divorce and Matrimonial Causes.
[*28 August 1860*]

* The whole Act was repealed by Supreme Court of Judicature (Consolidation) Act 1925, Sch 6, although much of it had already been repealed, as indicated in the notes to the various sections. The preamble was repealed by Statute Law Revision Act 1892 (55 and 56 Vict c 19).

1. The Judge Ordinary may exercise powers now vested in the full Court. *It shall be lawful for the Judge Ordinary of the Court for Divorce and Matrimonial Causes alone to hear and determine all matters arising in the said Court, and to exercise all powers and authority whatever which may now be heard and determined and exercised respectively by the full Court or by three or more judges of the said Court, the Judge Ordinary being one, or where the Judge Ordinary shall deem it expedient in relation to any matter which he might hear and determine alone by virtue of this Act, to have the assistance of one other judge of the said Court, it shall be lawful for the Judge Ordinary to sit and act with such one other judge accordingly, and, in conjunction with such other judge, to exercise all the jurisdiction, powers, and authority of the said Court.*

Note. Repealed by Statute Law Revision Act 1892 and by Supreme Court of Judicature (Consolidation) Act 1925, Sch 6.

2. Judge may direct any matter to be heard by the full Court. *Provided always, that the Judge Ordinary may, where he shall deem it expedient, direct that any such matter as aforesaid shall be heard and determined by the full Court; and in addition to the cases in which an appeal to the full Court now lies from the decision of the Judge Ordinary, either party dissatisfied with the decision of such Judge sitting alone in granting or refusing any application for a new trial which by virtue of this Act he is empowered to hear and determine may, within fourteen days after the pronouncing thereof, appeal to the full Court, whose decision shall be final.*

Note. Repealed by Statute Law Revision Act 1892 and by Supreme Court of Judicature (Consolidation) Act 1925, Sch 6. The Supreme Court of Judicature Act 1881, s 9, is partly repealed and re-enacted by Supreme Court of Judicature (Consolidation) Act 1925, s 27.

3. Appeal to the House of Lords. *Where there is a right of appeal to the House of Lords from the decision of the full Court there shall be the like right of appeal to the said House from the decision of the Judge Ordinary alone, or with any other judge, under this Act.*

Note. Repealed by Matrimonial Causes Act 1868, s 2 and by Supreme Court of Judicature (Consolidation) Act 1925, Sch 6.

4. (*Regulation of the sittings of the full Court: Matrimonial Causes Act 1859, s 2, repealed.*)

Note. Partly repealed by Statute Law Revision Act 1875, and, wholly, by Statute Law Revision Act 1892 and by Supreme Court of Judicature (Consolidation) Act 1925, Sch 6: see Administration of Justice (Appeals) Act 1934 (p 2086).

For Matrimonial Causes Act 1859, s 2, see p 2018.

5. Court may, where one party only appears, require counsel to be appointed to argue on the other side. *In every case of a petition for a dissolution of marriage it shall be lawful for the Court, if it shall see fit, to direct all necessary papers in the matter to be sent to Her Majesty's Proctor, who shall, under the directions of the Attorney-General, instruct counsel to argue before the Court any question in relation to such matter, and which the Court may deem it necessary or expedient to have fully argued; and Her Majesty's Proctor shall be entitled to charge and be reimbursed the costs of such proceeding as part of the expense of his office.*

Note. Repealed by Supreme Court of Judicature (Consolidation) Act 1925, Sch 6. See now Matrimonial Causes Act 1973, s 8(1) (p 2475), replacing Matrimonial Causes Act 1965, s 6(1) (p 2227), replacing Matrimonial Causes Act 1950, s 10 (p 2124), replacing Act of 1925, s 181 (p 2056).

6. 20 & 21 Vict c 85, s 45, amended. *And whereas by section forty-five of the Act of the session holden in the twentieth and twenty-first year of her Majesty, chapter eighty-five, it was enacted, that 'In any case in which the Court should pronounce a sentence of divorce or judicial separation for adultery of the wife, if it should be made appear to the Court that the wife was entitled to any property, either in possession or reversion, it should be lawful for the Court, if it should think proper, to order such settlement as it should think reasonable to be made of such property, or any part thereof, for the benefit of the innocent party and of the children of the marriage, or either of them': Be it further enacted, that any instrument executed pursuant to any order of the Court made under the said enactment before or after the passing of this Act, at the time of or after the pronouncing of a final decree of divorce or judicial separation, shall be deemed valid and effectual in the law, notwithstanding the existence of the disability of coverture at the time of the execution thereof.*

Note. Partly repealed by Statute Law Revision Act 1892: and wholly, by Supreme Court of Judicature (Consolidation) Act 1925, Sch 6. See now Matrimonial Causes Act 1973, ss 24, 25 (pp 2488, 2489), replacing Matrimonial Proceedings and Property Act 1970, ss 4, 5 (pp 2346, 2347), replacing Matrimonial Causes Act 1965, ss 17(2), 20(2), 21(3) (pp 2232, 2233), replacing Matrimonial Causes Act 1950, s 24 (p 2130), replacing s 191 of the Act of 1925 (p 2061), and Matrimonial Causes Act 1937, s 10 (p 2091).

For Matrimonial Causes Act 1857, s 45, see p 2010.

7. Decrees. *Every decree for a divorce shall in the first instance be a decree nisi, not to be made absolute till after the expiration of such time, not less than three months from the pronouncing thereof, as the Court shall by general or special order from time to time direct; and during that period any person shall be at liberty, in such manner as the Court shall by general or special order in that behalf from time to time direct, to show cause why the said decree should not be made absolute by reason of the same having been obtained by collusion or by reason of material facts not brought before the Court; and, on cause being so shown, the Court shall deal with the case by making the decree absolute, or by reversing the decree nisi, or by requiring further inquiry, or otherwise as justice may require; and at any time during the progress of the cause or before the* *decree is made absolute any person may give information to Her Majesty's Proctor of any matter material to the due decision of the case, who may thereupon take such steps as the Attorney-General may deem necessary or expedient; and if from any such information or otherwise the said Proctor shall suspect that any parties to the suit are or have been acting in collusion for the purpose of obtaining a divorce contrary to the justice of the case, he may, under the direction of the Attorney-General, and by leave of the Court, intervene in the suit, alleging such case of collusion, and retain counsel and subpœna witnesses to prove it; and it shall be lawful for the Court to order the costs of such counsel and witnesses, and otherwise, arising from such intervention, to be paid by the parties or such of them as it shall see fit, including a wife if she have separate property; and in case the said Proctor shall not thereby be fully satisfied his reasonable costs, he shall be entitled to charge and be reimbursed the difference as part of the expense of his office.*

Note. Extended to decrees for nullity by Matrimonial Causes Act 1873, s 1 (p 2022); and repealed by Supreme Court of Judicature (Consolidation) Act 1925, Sch 6. See now Matrimonial Causes Act 1973, ss 1–10 (pp 2471–2476), replacing Divorce Reform Act 1969, ss 1–5 (pp 2319–2321), and Matrimonial Causes Act 1965, ss 5, 6, 7, 10 (pp 2225–2229), replacing Matrimonial Causes Act 1950, ss 10, 11, 12 (p 2124), as amended by Matrimonial Causes Act 1963, s 4, replacing Act of 1925, ss 181, 182, 183 (pp 2056–2057): s 182 having been amended by Matrimonial Causes Act 1937, s 9.

8. Continuance of Act. *This Act shall continue in force until the thirty-first day of July one thousand eight hundred and sixty-two, and no longer.*

Note. 'Perpetuated' by Perpetuation of Matrimonial Causes Act 1860 Act 1862, passed expressly for that purpose; and wholly repealed by Supreme Court of Judicature (Consolidation) Act 1925, Sch 6.

MATRIMONIAL CAUSES ACT 1864*

(27 & 28 Vict c 44)

An Act to amend the Act relating to divorce and matrimonial causes in England, twentieth and twenty-first Victoria, chapter eighty-five.†

[*14 July 1864*]

1*. Amending provisions of 20 & 21 Vict c 85,† **as to orders of protection of property of wife deserted by her husband.** *Where under the provisions of section twenty-one of the said Act† a wife deserted by her husband shall have obtained or shall hereafter obtain an order protecting her earnings and property, from a police magistrate, or justices in petty sessions, or the Court for Divorce and Matrimonial Causes, as the case may be, the husband, and any creditor or other person claiming under him may apply to the Court or to the magistrate or justices by whom such order was made, for the discharge thereof as by the said Act authorised; and in case the said order shall have been made by a police magistrate and the said magistrate shall have died or been removed, or have become incapable of acting, then in every such case the husband or creditor, or such other person as aforesaid, may apply to the magistrate for the time being acting as the successor or in the place of the magistrate who made the order of protection, for the discharge of it, who shall have authority to make an order discharging the same; and an order for discharge of an order for protection may be applied for to and be granted by the Court, although the order for protection was not made by the Court, and an order for protection made at one petty sessions may be discharged by the justices of any later petty sessions, or by the Court.*

* Partly repealed for all purposes and wholly repealed, so far as it related to the High Court, by Supreme Court of Judicature (Consolidation) Act 1925, Sch 6 and finally repealed for all purposes by Administration of Justice Act 1965, s 34, Sch 2.

† Ie Matrimonial Causes Act 1857, s 21 (p 2004).

MATRIMONIAL CAUSES ACT 1866‡

(29 & 30 Vict c 32)

An Act further to amend the procedure and powers of the Court for Divorce and Matrimonial Causes.

[*11 June 1866*]

‡ This Act was repealed by Supreme Court of Judicature (Consolidation) Act 1925, Sch 6.

Whereas by the Act passed in the session of parliament holden in the twentieth and twenty-first years of the reign of her present Majesty intituled An Act to amend the laws relating to Divorce and Matrimonial Causes in England, it is by the thirty-second section enacted, 'that the Court may, on pronouncing any decree for a dissolution of marriage, order that the husband shall to the satisfaction of the Court secure to the wife such gross or annual sum of money as to the Court may seem reasonable, and for that purpose may refer it to one of the conveyancing counsel of the Court of Chancery to settle and approve of a proper deed to be executed by all necessary parties:'

And whereas it sometimes happens that a decree for a dissolution of marriage is obtained against a husband who has no property on which the payments of any such gross or annual sum can be secured, but nevertheless he would be able to make a monthly or weekly payment to the wife during their joint lives:

Be it therefore enacted, etc.

1. Power to order monthly or weekly payments to wife from husband on dissolution of marriage. *In every such case it shall be lawful for the Court to make an order on the husband for payment to the wife during their joint lives of such monthly or weekly sums for her maintenance and support as the Court may think reasonable: Provided always, that if the husband shall afterwards from any cause become unable to make such payments it shall be lawful for the Court to discharge or modify the order, or temporarily to suspend the same as to the whole or any part of the money so ordered to be paid and again to revive the same order, wholly or in part, as to the Court may seem fit.*

Note. Repealed by the Matrimonial Causes Act 1907, s 2. See now Matrimonial Causes Act 1973, ss 22, 23, 25, 27 (pp 2482, 2484, 2489, 2496), replacing Matrimonial Proceedings and Property Act 1970, ss 1, 3, 5, 7 (pp 2345, 2346, 2347, 2349), replacing Matrimonial Causes Act 1965, ss 15, 16, 19, 20(1), (2) (pp 2230–2232), replacing Matrimonial Causes Act 1950, ss 19, 20, 22 (pp 2128, 2129), replacing Supreme Court of Judicature (Consolidation) Act 1925, s 190 (p 2060).

2. In cases of opposition on certain grounds. *In any suit instituted for dissolution of marriage, if the respondent shall oppose the relief sought on the ground in case of such a suit instituted by a husband of his adultery, cruelty, or desertion, or in case of such a suit instituted by a wife on the ground of her adultery or cruelty, the Court may in such suit give to the respondent, on his or her application, the same relief to which he or she would have been entitled in case he or she had filed a petition seeking such relief.*

Note. Repealed by Supreme Court of Judicature (Consolidation) Act 1925, Sch 6. See now Matrimonial Causes Act 1973, s 20 (p 2481), replacing Matrimonial Causes Act 1965, s 5(6) (p 2226), replacing Matrimonial Causes Act 1950, s 6 (p 2122), replacing Act of 1925, s 180 (p 2060).

3. Decree nisi not absolute till after 6 months. *No decree nisi for a divorce shall be made absolute until after the expiration of six calendar months from the pronouncing thereof, unless the Court shall under the power now vested in it fix a shorter time.*

Note. Extended to nullity decrees by Matrimonial Causes Act 1873, s 1 (p 2022); repealed by Supreme Court of Judicature (Consolidation) Act 1925, Sch 6. See now Matrimonial Causes Act 1973, s 1(5) (p 2471), replacing Matrimonial Causes Act 1965, s 5(7) (p 2226), replacing Matrimonial Causes Act 1950, s 12 (p 2124), replacing Act of 1925, s 183 (p 2057), as amended by Matrimonial Causes Act 1937, s 9.

MATRIMONIAL CAUSES ACT 1868*

(31 & 32 Vict c 77)

An Act to amend the law relating to appeals from the Court of Divorce and Matrimonial Causes in England. [*31 July 1868*]

    * This Act was repealed by Supreme Court of Judicature (Consolidation) Act 1925, Sch 6.

1. (*Interpretation.*)
Note. Repealed by Statute Law Revision Act 1893.

2. *Matrimonial Causes Act 1857 (20 & 21 Vict c 85), s 56; Matrimonial Causes Act 1858 (21 & 22 Vict c 108), s 17; and Matrimonial Causes Act 1860 (23 & 24 Vict c 144), s 3, repealed.*
Note. Repealed by Statute Law Revision Act 1875.
    For Matrimonial Causes Act 1857, s 56, see p 2012.
    For Matrimonial Causes Act 1858, s 17, see p 2017.
    For Matrimonial Causes Act 1860, s 3, see p 2020.

3. Appeals to House of Lords to be within one month. *Either party dissatisfied with the final decision of the Court on any petition for dissolution or nullity of marriage may, within one calendar month after the pronouncing thereof, appeal therefrom to the House of Lords, and on the hearing of any such appeal the House of Lords may either dismiss the appeal or reverse the decree, or remit the case to be dealt with in all respects as the House of Lords shall direct: Provided always, that in suits for dissolution of marriage no respondent or co-respondent, not appearing and defending the suit on the occasion of the decree nisi being made, shall have any right of appeal to the House of Lords against a decree when made absolute, unless the Court, upon application made at the time of the pronouncing of the decree absolute, shall see fit to permit an appeal.*
Note. Repealed by Statute Law Revision Act 1893. See Supreme Court of Judicature Act 1881, ss 9, 10; and, now, Supreme Court Act 1981, ss 16, 18(1)(d) (pp 2775, 2776).

4. Liberty to parties to marry again. *Section fifty-seven of the said Act of twenty-first Victoria, chapter eighty-five, shall be read and construed with reference to the time for appealing as varied by this Act; and in cases where under this Act there shall be no right of appeal, the parties respectively shall be at liberty to marry again at any time after the pronouncing of the decree absolute.*
Note. Partly repealed by Statute Law Revision Act 1893 and, wholly, by Supreme Court of Judicature (Consolidation) Act, 1925, Sch 6. See now Supreme Court Act 1981, ss 16, 18(1)(d) (pp 2775, 2776), and Matrimonial Causes Act 1965, s 8(2) (p 2228), replacing Matrimonial Causes Act 1950, s 13(2) (p 2125), replacing Matrimonial Causes Act 1937, s 12 (p 2093).
    For Matrimonial Causes Act 1857, s 57, see p 2012.

5. Short title. *This Act may be cited as 'the Divorce Amendment Act 1868.'*
Note. But, by the Matrimonial Causes Act 1873, s 2 (p 2022), it could be cited as the Matrimonial Causes Act 1868.

6. (*Qualified retrospective operation.*)
Note. Partly repealed by Statute Law Revision Act 1875, and, wholly, by Statute Law Revision Act 1893.

DEBTORS ACT 1869

32 & 33 Vict c 62

An Act for the Abolition of Imprisonment for Debt, for the punishment of fraudulent debtors, and for other purposes. [9 August 1869]

Preliminary

1.   Short title. This Act may be cited for all purposes as 'The Debtors Act 1869'.

2.   Extent. This Act shall not extend to Scotland or Ireland.

3.   Construction. ... Words and expressions defined or explained in the Bankruptcy Act 1869 shall have the same meaning in this Act.
Note. Words omitted repealed by Statute Law Revision (No 2) Act 1893.

PART I

ABOLITION OF IMPRISONMENT FOR DEBT

4.   Abolition of imprisonment for debt, with exceptions. With the exceptions herein-after mentioned, no person shall ... be arrested or imprisoned for making default in payment of a sum of money.
There shall be excepted from the operation of the above enactment:
1.   Default in payment of a penalty, or sum in the nature of a penalty, other than a penalty in respect of any contract:
2.   Default in payment of any sum recoverable summarily before a justice or justices of the peace:
3.   Default by a trustee or person acting in a fiduciary capacity and ordered to pay by a court of equity any sum in his possession or under his control:
4.   Default by any attorney or solicitor in payment of costs when ordered to pay costs for misconduct as such, or in payment of a sum of money when ordered to pay the same in his character of an officer of the court making the order:
5.   Default in payment for the benefit of creditors of any portion of a salary or other income in respect of the payment of which any court having jurisdiction in bankruptcy is authorised to make an order:
6.   Default in payment of sums in respect of the payment of which orders are in this Act authorised to be made:
Provided, first, that no person shall be imprisoned in any case excepted from the operation of this section for a longer period than one year; and, secondly, that nothing in this section shall alter the effect of any judgment or order of any court for payment of money except as regards the arrest and imprisonment of the person making default in paying such money.
Note. Words omitted repealed by Statute Law Revision (No 2) Act 1893.

5.   Saving of power of committal for small debts. Subject to the provisions herein-after mentioned, and to the prescribed rules, any court may commit to prison for a term not exceeding six weeks, or until payment of the sum due, any person who makes default in payment of any debt or instalment of any debt due from him in pursuance of any order or judgment of that or any other competent court.
Provided—(1) That the jurisdiction by this section given of committing a person to prison shall, in the case of any court other than the superior courts of law and equity, be exercised only subject to the following restrictions; that is to say,
(a)   Be exercised only by a judge or his deputy, and by an order made in open court and showing on its face the ground on which it is issued:
(b)   ...
(c)   Be exercised only as respects a judgment of a county court by a county court judge or his deputy.
(2)   That such jurisdiction shall only be exercised where it is proved to the satisfaction of the court that the person making default either has or has had since the date of the order or judgment the means to pay the sum in respect of which he has made default, and has refused or neglected, or refuses or neglects, to pay the same.

Proof of the means of the person making default may be given in such manner as the court thinks just; and for the purposes of such proof the debtor and any witnesses may be summoned and examined on oath, according to the prescribed rules.

Any jurisdiction by this section given to the superior courts may be exercised by a judge sitting in chambers, or otherwise, in the prescribed manner.

For the purposes of this section any court may direct any debt due from any person in pursuance of any order or judgment of that or any other competent court to be paid by instalments, and may from time to time rescind or vary such order:

Persons committed under this section by a superior court may be committed to the prison in which they would have been confined if arrested on a writ of capias ad satisfaciendum, and every order of committal by any superior court shall, subject to the prescribed rules, be issued, obeyed, and executed in the like manner as such writ.

This section, so far as it relates to any county court, shall be deemed to be substituted for sections ninety-eight and ninety-nine of the County Courts Act 1846 and that Act and the Acts amending the same shall be construed accordingly, and shall extend to orders made by the county court with respect to sums due in pursuance of any order or judgment of any court other than a county court.

No imprisonment under this section shall operate as a satisfaction or extinguishment of any debt or demand or cause of action, or deprive any person of any right to take out execution against the lands, goods, or chattels of the person imprisoned, in the same manner as if such imprisonment had not taken place.

Any person imprisoned under this section shall be discharged out of custody upon a certificate signed in the prescribed manner to the effect that he has satisfied a debt or instalment of a debt in respect of which he was imprisoned, together with the prescribed costs (if any).

Note. Words omitted repealed by Bankruptcy Act 1883, s 169(1), Sch 5. Modified by Administration of Justice Act 1970, s 11, Sch 4.

6.   Arrest of defendant about to quit England. ... Where the plaintiff in any action in any of Her Majesty's superior courts of law at Westminster in which, if brought before the commencement of this Act, the defendant would have been liable to arrest, proves at any time before final judgment by evidence on oath, to the satisfaction of a judge of one of those courts, that the plaintiff has good cause of action against the defendant to the amount of fifty pounds or upwards, and that there is probable cause for believing that the defendant is about to quit England unless he be apprehended, and that the absence of the defendant from England will materially prejudice the plaintiff in the prosecution of his action, such judge may in the prescribed manner order such defendant to be arrested and imprisoned for a period not exceeding six months, unless and until he has sooner given the prescribed security, not exceeding the amount claimed in the action, that he will not go out of England without the leave of the court.

Where the action is for a penalty or sum in the nature of a penalty other than a penalty in respect of any contract, it shall not be necessary to prove that the absence of the defendant from England will materially prejudice the plaintiff in the prosecution of his action, and the security given (instead of being that the defendant will not go out of England) shall be to the effect that any sum recovered against the defendant in the action shall be paid, or that the defendant shall be rendered to prison.

Note. Words omitted repealed by Statute Law Revision (No 2) Act 1893.

*   *   *   *   *

8.   Saving for sequestration against property. Sequestration against the property of a debtor may ... be issued by any court of equity in the same manner as if such debtor had been actually arrested.

Note. Words omitted repealed by Statute Law Revision (No 2) Act 1893.

*   *   *   *   *

10.   Definition of 'prescribed'. In this part of this Act the term 'prescribed' means as follows:—

As respects the superior courts of common law, prescribed by general rules to be made in pursuance of the Common Law Procedure Act 1852;

As respects the superior courts of equity prescribed by general rules and orders to be made in pursuance of the Court of Chancery Act 1852;

As respects the county courts, prescribed by general rules to be made under the County Courts Act 1856; and

...

And general rules and orders may respectively be made by such authorities as aforesaid, for the purpose of carrying into effect this part of this Act.

Note. Words omitted repealed by Courts Act 1971, s 56(4), Sch 11, Part IV. This section repealed as respects courts of summary jurisdiction by Justices of the Peace Act 1949, s 46(2), Sch 7, Part II.

*   *   *   *   *

PART II

PUNISHMENT OF FRAUDULENT DEBTORS

13.   Penalty on fraudulently obtaining credit, etc. Any person shall in each of the cases following be deemed guilty of a misdemeanour, and on conviction thereof shall be liable to be imprisoned for any time not exceeding one year, with or without hard labour; that is to say,

(1) ...

(2) If he has with intent to defraud his creditors, or any of them, made or caused to be made any gift, delivery, or transfer of or any charge on his property:

(3) If he has, with intent to defraud his creditors, concealed or removed any part of his property since or within two months before the date of any unsatisfied judgment or order for payment of money obtained against him.

Note. Words omitted repealed by Theft Act 1968, ss 33(3), 35, Sch 3, Part I.

EVIDENCE FURTHER AMENDMENT ACT 1869

(32 & 33 Vict c 68)

[*9 August 1869*]

3. Parties and their husbands and wives to be witnesses in suits for adultery.
The parties to any proceeding instituted in consequence of adultery, and the husbands and wives of such parties, shall be competent to give evidence in such proceeding; Provided that no witness in any proceeding, whether a party to the suit or not, shall be liable to be asked or bound to answer any question tending to show that he or she has been guilty of adultery, unless such witness shall have already given evidence in the same proceeding in disproof of his or her alleged adultery.

Note. Repealed by Supreme Court of Judicature (Consolidation) Act 1925, Sch 6 'so far as it relates to the High Court': see ibid s 198 (p 2064) and the note thereto. Wholly repealed except as to Northern Ireland, by Statute Law (Repeals) Act 1978, and as to Northern Ireland, by SI 1984 No 1984.

MATRIMONIAL CAUSES ACT 1873*

(36 & 37 Vict c 31)

An Act to extend to suits for nullity of marriage the law with respect to the intervention of Her Majesty's Proctor and others in suits in England for dissolving marriages.   [*16 June 1873*]

* This Act was repealed by the Supreme Court of Judicature (Consolidation) Act 1925, Sch 6.

Whereas under section seven of the Act of the session of the twenty-third and twenty-fourth years of the reign of Her present Majesty, chapter one hundred and forty-four, intituled 'An Act to amend the procedure and powers of the Court for Divorce and Matrimonial Causes' [ie the Matrimonial Causes Act, 1860 (23 & 24 Vict c 144), s 7], and under section three of the Act of the session of the twenty-ninth and thirtieth years of the reign of Her present Majesty, chapter thirty-two, intituled 'An Act further to amend the procedure and powers of the Court for Divorce and Matrimonial Causes' [ie the Matrimonial Causes Act, 1866 (29 & 30 Vict c 32), s 3], a decree for divorce is required in the first instance to be a decree nisi, and not to be made absolute until after the expiration of six months, unless the Court otherwise direct, and provision is made for any person showing cause why the decree should not be made absolute by reason of the same having been obtained by collusion, or of material facts not having been brought before the Court, and power is given to any person to give information to Her Majesty's Proctor, who is thereupon authorised to take such steps as the Attorney-General may deem necessary or expedient, and such Proctor, if he suspects that any parties to the suit are acting in collusion for the purpose of obtaining a divorce contrary to the justice of the case, is authorised under the direction of the Attorney-General and by leave of the Court to intervene in the suit, and otherwise proceed as therein mentioned, and provision is made for the payment of his costs in so acting:

And whereas it is expedient to extend such provisions to a suit for nullity of marriage:

Be it therefore enacted, etc.

Note. Preamble repealed by Statute Law Revision (No 2) Act 1893.
For Matrimonial Causes Act 1860, s 7, see p 2020.
For Matrimonial Causes Act 1866, s 3, see p 2022.

1. Extension of s 7 of [Matrimonial Causes Act 1860] 23 & 24 Vict c 144, and s 3 of [Matrimonial Causes Act 1866] 29 & 30 Vict c 32, to suits for nullity of marriage. *The above-mentioned sections of the said Acts shall extend to decrees and suits for nullity of marriage in like manner as they apply to decrees and suits for divorce, and shall be construed as if they were herein enacted, with the substitution of the words 'a decree for nullity of marriage' for the words 'decree for a divorce' or 'divorce,' as the case may require.*

Note. Repealed by Supreme Court of Judicature (Consolidation) Act 1925, Sch 6. See now Matrimonial Causes Act 1973, ss 1(5), 8, 9, 15 (pp 2471, 2475, 2478), replacing Matrimonial Causes Act 1965, ss 5(7), 6, 7, 10 (pp 2225–2227, 2229), replacing Matrimonial Causes Act 1950, ss 10, 11, 12 (p 2124), replacing Act of 1925, ss 181, 182, 183 (pp 2056, 2057), and Matrimonial Causes Act 1937, s 9 (p 2091).

2. Short title. *This Act, together with the Acts specified in the schedule to this Act, may be cited as 'the Matrimonial Causes Acts, 1857 to 1873,' and each Act may be cited as the Matrimonial Causes Act of the year in which it was passed.*

Note. Partly repealed (together with the Schedule which detailed the previous Acts) by Statute Law Revision (No 2) Act 1893, and, wholly, by Supreme Court of Judicature (Consolidation) Act 1925, Sch 6.

SUPREME COURT OF JUDICATURE ACT 1873
(36 & 37 Vict c 66)

[*5 August 1873*]

23. Rules as to exercise of jurisdiction. *The jurisdiction by this Act transferred to the said High Court of Justice and the said Court of Appeal respectively shall be exercised (so far as regards procedure and practice) in the manner provided by this Act, or by such Rules and Orders of Court as may be made pursuant to this Act; and where no special provision is contained in this Act or in any such Rules or Orders of Court with reference thereto, it shall be exercised as nearly as may be in the same manner as the same might have been exercised by the respective Courts from which such jurisdiction shall have been transferred, or by any of such Courts.*

Note. Repealed and replaced by Supreme Court of Judicature Act 1925, s 32 (repealed: see note thereto).

MATRIMONIAL CAUSES ACT 1878*

(41 & 42 Vict c 19)

An Act to amend the Matrimonial Causes Acts. [*27 May 1878*]

   * This Act was repealed by Supreme Court of Judicature (Consolidation) Act 1925, Sch 6.

1. Short title. *This Act may be cited as the Matrimonial Causes Act 1878.*

2. Costs of intervention. *Where the Queen's Proctor or any other person shall intervene or show cause against a decree nisi in any suit or proceedings for divorce or for nullity of marriage, the Court may make such order as to the costs of the Queen's Proctor, or of any other person who shall intervene or show cause as aforesaid, or of all and every party or parties thereto, occasioned by such intervention or showing cause as aforesaid, as may seem just; and the Queen's Proctor, any other person as aforesaid, and such party or parties shall be entitled to recover such costs in like manner as in other cases: Provided that the Treasury may, if it shall think fit, order any costs which the Queen's Proctor shall, by any order of the Court made under this section, pay to the said party or parties, to be deemed to be part of the expenses of his office.*

Note. Repealed by Supreme Court of Judicature (Consolidation) Act 1925, Sch 6. See now Matrimonial Causes Act 1973, ss 8, 15 (pp 2475, 2478), replacing Matrimonial Causes Act 1965, ss 6, 10 (pp 2227, 2229), replacing Matrimonial Causes Act 1950, s 11 (p 2124), replacing Act of 1925, s 182 (p 2057).

3. Extension of power given by [Matrimonial Causes Act, 1859]. *The Court may exercise the powers vested in it by the provisions of section five of the Act of the twenty-second and twenty-third years of Victoria, chapter sixty-one, notwithstanding that there are no children of the marriage.*

Note. Ie the power to vary ante-nuptial and post-nuptial settlements after a final decree of divorce or nullity. Repealed by Supreme Court of Judicature (Consolidation) Act 1925, Sch 6. See now Matrimonial Causes Act 1973, ss 24, 25, 51(1) (pp 2487, 2489, 2525), replacing Matrimonial Proceedings and Property Act 1970, ss 4, 5, 27(1) (pp 2346, 2347, 2359), replacing Matrimonial Causes Act 1965, ss 17(1), 19, 46(2) (pp 2231, 2232, 2249), replacing Matrimonial Causes Act 1950, s 25 (p 2131), replacing Act of 1925, s 192 (p 2062.)

   For Matrimonial Causes Act 1859, s 5, see p 2018.

4. If husband convicted of aggravated assault, Court may order that wife be not bound to cohabit, &c. *If a husband shall be convicted summarily or otherwise of an aggravated assault within the meaning of the statute twenty-fourth and twenty-fifth Victoria, chapter one hundred, section forty-three, upon his wife, the Court or magistrate before whom he shall be so convicted may, if satisfied that the future safety of the wife is in peril, order that the wife shall be no longer bound to cohabit with her husband; and such order shall have the force and effect in all respects of a decree of judicial separation on the ground of cruelty; and such order may further provide.*

   (*1*) *That the husband shall pay to his wife such weekly sum as the Court or magistrate may consider to be in accordance with his means, and with any means which the wife may have for her support, and the payment of any sum of money so ordered shall be enforceable and enforced against the husband in the same manner as the payment of money is enforced under an order of affiliation; and the Court or magistrate by whom any such order for payment of money shall be made shall have power from time to time to vary the same on the application of either the husband or the wife, upon proof that the means of the husband or wife have been altered in amount since the original order or any subsequent order varying it shall have been made;*

   (*2*) *That the legal custody of any children of the marriage under the age of ten years shall, in the discretion of the Court or magistrate be given to the wife.*

   Provided always, that no order for payment of money by the husband or for the custody of children by the wife, shall be made in favour of a wife who shall be proved to have committed adultery, unless such adultery has been condoned; and that any order for payment of money or for the custody of children may be discharged by the Court or magistrate by whom such order was made upon proof that the wife has since the making thereof been guilty of adultery; and provided also, that all orders made under this section shall be subject to appeal to the Probate and Admiralty Division [sic] *of the High Court of Justice.*

Note. Repealed by Summary Jurisdiction (Married Women) Act 1895, s 12.

BANKERS' BOOKS EVIDENCE ACT 1879

(42 & 43 Vict c 11)

An Act to amend the Law of Evidence with respect to Bankers' Books. [23 May 1879]

1. Short title. This Act may be cited as the Bankers' Books Evidence Act 1879.

2. ...

Note. This section repealed by Statute Law Revision Act 1894.

3. Mode of proof of entries in bankers' books. Subject to the provisions of this Act, a copy of any entry in a banker's book shall in all legal proceedings be received as primâ facie evidence of such entry, and of the matters, transactions, and accounts therein recorded.

4. Proof that book is a banker's book. A copy of an entry in a banker's book shall not be received in evidence under this Act unless it be first proved that the book was at the time of the making of the entry one of the ordinary books of the bank, and that the entry was made in the usual and ordinary course of business, and that the book is in the custody or control of the bank.

Such proof may be given by a partner or officer of the bank, and may be given orally or by an affidavit sworn before any commissioner or person authorised to take affidavits.

[Where the proceedings concerned are proceedings before a magistrates' court inquiring into an offence as examining justices, this section shall have effect with the omission of the words 'orally or'.]

Note. Words in square brackets added by Criminal Procedure and Investigations Act 1996, s 47, Sch 1, para 15, as from 4 July 1996, with effect from a day to be appointed.

5. Verification of copy. A copy of an entry in a banker's book shall not be received in evidence under this Act unless it be further proved that the copy has been examined with the original entry and is correct.

Such proof shall be given by some person who has examined the copy with the original entry, and may be given either orally or by an affidavit sworn before any commissioner or person authorised to take affidavits.

[Where the proceedings concerned are proceedings before a magistrates' court inquiring into an offence as examining justices, this section shall have effect with the omission of the words 'orally or'.]

Note. Words in square brackets added by Criminal Procedure and Investigations Act 1996, s 47, Sch 1, para 16, as from 4 July 1996, with effect in relation to any alleged offence into which no criminal investigation has begun before 1 April 1997.

6. Case in which banker, etc, not compellable to produce book, etc. A banker or officer of a bank shall not, in any legal proceeding to which the bank is not a party, be compellable to produce any banker's book the contents of which can be proved under this Act [or under the Civil Evidence (Scotland) Act 1988] [or Schedule 8 to the Criminal Procedure (Scotland) Act 1995] [or Schedule 3 to the Prisoners and Criminal Proceedings (Scotland) Act 1993], or to appear as a witness to prove the matters, transactions, and accounts therein recorded, unless by order of a judge made for special cause.

Note. Words in first pair of square brackets inserted by Civil Evidence (Scotland) Act 1988, s 73, as from 3 April 1989. Words in second pair of square brackets inserted by Criminal Procedure (Consequential Provisions) (Scotland) Act 1995, s 5, Sch 4, para 2, as from 1 April 1996. Words in third pair of square brackets inserted by Prisoners and Criminal Proceedings (Scotland) Act 1993, s 29, Sch 3, para 7(3), as from 1 October 1993.

7. Court or judge may order inspection, etc. On the application of any party to a legal proceeding a court or judge may order that such party be at liberty to inspect and take copies of any entries in a banker's book for any of the purposes of such proceedings. An order under this section may be made either with or without summoning the bank or any other party, and shall be served on the bank three clear days before the same is to be obeyed, unless the court or judge otherwise directs.

8. Costs. The costs of any application to a court or judge or for the purposes of this Act, and the costs of anything done or to be done under an order of a court or judge made under or for the purposes of this Act shall be in the discretion of the court or judge, who may order the same or any part thereof to be paid to any party by the bank where the same have been occasioned by any default or delay on the part of the bank. Any such order against a bank may be enforced as if the bank was a party to the proceeding.

[9. Interpretation of 'bank', 'banker', and 'bankers' book'—(1) In this Act the expressions 'bank' and 'banker' mean—

    [(a) *a recognised bank, licensed institution or municipal bank, within the meaning of the Banking Act 1979;*

    [(a) an institution authorised under the Banking Act 1987 or a municipal bank within the meaning of that Act;]

    [(aa) a building society (within the meaning of the Building Societies Act 1986);]

    [(b) *a trustee savings bank within the meaning of [the Trustee Savings Banks Act 1981];*

    [(c) the National Savings Bank; and

    [(d) the Post Office, in the exercise of its powers to provide banking services.

    (2) Expressions in this Act relating to 'bankers' books' include ledgers, day books, cash books, account books and other records used in the ordinary business of the bank, whether those records are in written form or are kept on microfilm, magnetic tape or any form of mechanical or electronic data retrieval mechanism.]

Note. This section substituted by Banking Act 1979, s 51(1), Sch 6, Part I, para 1, as from 19 February 1982, and sub-s (1)(b) further amended by Trustee Savings Bank Act 1981, s 55(1), Sch 6. Sub-s (1)(b) repealed by Trustee Savings Banks Act 1985, ss 4(3), 7(4), Sch 4. Sub-s (1)(a) substituted by Banking Act 1987, s 108(1), Sch 6, para 1. Sub-s 1(aa) inserted by Building Societies Act 1986, s 120(1), Sch 18, Part I, para 1, as from 1 January 1987.

10. Interpretation of 'legal proceeding', 'court', 'judge'. In this Act—

    The expression 'legal proceeding' means any civil or criminal proceeding or inquiry in which evidence is or may be given, and includes *an arbitration [and an application to, or an inquiry or other proceeding before the Solicitors Disciplinary Tribunal or any body exercising functions in relation to solicitors in Scotland or Northern Ireland corresponding to the functions of that Tribunal]*;

    [(a) an arbitration;

    (b) an application to, or an inquiry or other proceeding before, the Solicitors Disciplinary Tribunal or any body exercising functions in relation to solicitors in Scotland or Northern Ireland corresponding to the functions of that Tribunal; and

    (c) an investigation of a complaint by the adjudicator of a recognised scheme for the purposes of section 83 of the Building Societies Act 1986.]

    The expression 'the court' means the court, judge, arbitrator, persons or person before whom a legal proceeding is held or taken;

    The expression 'a judge' means with respect to England a judge of the High Court ... , and with respect to Scotland a lord ordinary of the Outer House of the

Court of Session, and with respect to Ireland a judge of the High Court ... in Ireland;

The judge of a county court may with respect to any action in such court exercise the powers of a judge under this Act.

Note. The words omitted repealed by Statute Law Revision Act 1898. First words in square brackets inserted by Solicitors Act 1974, s 86. Words in italics repealed and subsequent words in square brackets substituted by the Building Societies Act 1997, s 45(1), as from 9 June 1997.

11. Computation of time. Sunday, Christmas Day, Good Friday, and any bank holiday shall be excluded from the computation of time under this Act.

MARRIED WOMEN'S PROPERTY ACT 1882

(45 & 46 Vict c 75)

12. Remedies of married woman for protection and security of separate property. *Every woman, whether married before or after this Act, shall have in her own name against all persons whomsoever, including her husband, the same civil remedies, and also (subject, as regards her husband, to the proviso hereinafter contained) the same remedies and redress by way of criminal proceedings, for the protection and security of her own separate property, as if such property belonged to her as* [*she were*] *a feme sole, but, except as aforesaid, no husband or wife shall be entitled to sue the other for a tort. In any indictment or other proceeding under this section it shall be sufficient to allege such property to be her property; and in any proceeding under this section a husband or wife shall be competent to give evidence against each other, any statute or rule of law to the contrary notwithstanding: Provided always, that no criminal proceeding shall be taken by any wife against her husband by virtue of this Act while they are living together, as to or concerning any property claimed by her, nor while they are living apart, as to or concerning any act done by the husband while they were living together, concerning property claimed by the wife, unless such property shall have been wrongfully taken by the husband when leaving or deserting, or about to leave or desert, his wife.*

Note. Words in square brackets substituted by Law Reform (Married Women and Tortfeasors) Act 1935, s 5(1), First Schedule, for the original words 'such property belonged to her as'.

The whole section repealed, except so far as related to criminal proceedings, by Law Reform (Husband and Wife) Act 1962, s 3(2), Schedule, and repealed for all purposes by Theft Act 1968, s 33(3), Sch 3, Part III.

17. Questions between husband and wife as to property to be decided in a summary way. In any question between husband and wife as to the title to or possession of property, either party, *or any such bank, corporation, company, public body, or society as aforesaid in whose books any stocks, funds, or share of either party are standing,* may apply by summons or otherwise in a summary way [to the High Court or such county court as may be prescribed and the court may, on such an application (which may be heard in private), make such order with respect to the property as it thinks fit.

In this section 'prescribed' means prescribed by rules of court and rules made for the purposes of this section may confer jurisdiction on county courts whatever the situation or value of the property in dispute.] *to any judge of the High Court of Justice in England or in Ireland, according as such property is in England or Ireland, or (at the option of the applicant irrespectively of the value of the property in dispute) in England to the judge of the county court of the district, or in Ireland to the chairman of the civil bill court of the division in which either party resides, and the judge of the High Court of Justice or of the county court, or the chairman of the civil bill court (as the case may be) may make such order with respect to the property in dispute, and as to the costs of and consequent on the application as he thinks fit, or may direct such application to stand over from time to time, and any inquiry touching the matters in question to be made in such manner as he shall think fit: Provided always, that any order of a judge of the High Court of Justice to be made under the provisions of this section shall be subject to appeal in the same way as an order made by the same judge in a suit pending or on an equitable plaint in the said court would be; and any order of a county or civil bill court under the provisions of this section shall be subject to appeal in the same way as any other order made by the same court would be, and all proceedings in a county court or civil bill court under this section in which, by reason of the value of the property in dispute, such court would not have had jurisdiction if this Act or the Married Women's Property Act 1870, had not passed, may, at the option of the defendant or respondent to such proceedings, be removed as of right into the High Court of Justice in England or Ireland (as the case may be) by writ of certiorari or otherwise as may be prescribed by any rule of such High Court; but any order made or act done in the course of such proceedings prior to such removal shall be valid, unless order shall be made to the contrary by such High Court: Provided also, that the judge of the High Court of Justice or of the county court, or the chairman of the civil bill court, if either party so require, may hear any such application in his private room: Provided also, that any such bank, corporation, company, public body, or society as aforesaid, shall, in the matter of any such application for the purposes of costs or otherwise, be treated as a stakeholder only.*

Note. Words in italics 'or any such bank ... are standing' and 'Provided also ... as a stakeholder only' repealed as to England and Wales by Statute Law (Repeals) Act 1969, s 1, Schedule.

Words in italics 'to any judge of the High Court ... in his private room' substituted by words in square brackets by Matrimonial and Family Proceedings Act 1984, s 43.

For the extension of the court's powers under this section, see Matrimonial Causes (Property and Maintenance) Act 1958, s 7 (p 2188) and Matrimonial Proceedings and Property Act 1970, s 39 (p 2363). See also Law Reform (Husband and Wife) Act 1962 (p 2215) and Married Women's Property Act 1964 (p 2221).

For the application of this section to engaged couples where the agreement to marry is terminated, see Law Reform (Miscellaneous Provisions) Act 1970, s 2(2) (p 2341).

MATRIMONIAL CAUSES ACT 1884*

(47 & 48 Vict c 68)

An Act to amend the Matrimonial Causes Acts.   [*14 August 1884*]

* This Act was repealed by Supreme Court of Judicature (Consolidation) Act 1925.

1. Short title. *This Act may be cited as the Matrimonial Causes Act 1884.*

Note. But it was not referred to in the Matrimonial Causes Act 1907, s 4 (p 2035), as a Matrimonial Causes Act.

2. Periodical payments in lieu of attachment. *From and after the passing of this Act a decree for restitution of conjugal rights shall not be enforced by attachment, but where the application is by the wife the Court may, at the time of making such decree, or at any time afterwards, order that in the event of such decree not being complied with within any time in that behalf limited by the Court, the respondent shall make to the petitioner such periodical payments as may be just, and such order may be enforced in the same manner as an order for alimony in a suit for judicial separation. The Court may, if it shall think fit, order that the husband shall, to the satisfaction of the Court, secure to the wife such periodical payment, and for that purpose may refer it to any one of the Conveyancing Counsel of the Court to settle and approve of a proper deed or instrument to be executed by all necessary parties.*

Note. See Matrimonial Proceedings and Property Act 1970, ss 20, 42(2), Sch 3 (repealed) (pp 2357, 2364, 2368), repealing but not replacing Matrimonial Causes Act 1965, s 21(1), (2), (p 2233), replacing Matrimonial Causes Act 1950, s 22(3), (4) (p 2129), replacing Supreme Court of Judicature (Consolidation) Act 1925, s 187 (p 2059).

3. Settlement of wife's property. *Where the application for restitution of conjugal rights is by the husband, if it shall be made to appear to the Court that the wife is entitled to any property, either in possession or reversion, or is in receipt of any profits of trade or earnings, the Court may, if it shall think fit, order a settlement to be made to the satisfaction of the Court of such property, or any part thereof, for the benefit of the petitioner and of the children of the marriage, or either or any of them, or may order such part as the Court may think reasonable of such profits of trade or earnings to be periodically paid by the respondent to the petitioner for his own benefit, or to the petitioner or any other person for the benefit of the children of the marriage, or either or any of them.*

Note. See Matrimonial Proceedings and Property Act 1970, ss 20 (abolition of right to claim restitution of conjugal rights), 42(2), Sch 3 (repealed) (pp 2357, 2364, 2368), repealing but not replacing Matrimonial Causes Act 1965, s 21(3) (p 2233), replacing Matrimonial Causes

Act 1950, s 24 (p 2130), replacing Supreme Court of Judicature (Consolidation) Act 1925, s 191(2) (p 2061).

4. Power to vary orders. *The Court may from time to time vary or modify any order for the periodical payment of money, either by altering the times of payment or by increasing or diminishing the amount, or may temporarily suspend the same as to the whole or any part of the money so ordered to be paid and again revive the same order wholly or in part, as the Court may think just.*

Note. See now Matrimonial Causes Act 1973, s 31 (p 2503), replacing Matrimonial Proceedings and Property Act 1970, s 9 (p 2350), replacing Matrimonial Causes Act 1965, s 31 (p 2241), replacing Matrimonial Causes Act 1950, s 28 (p 2132).

5. Non-compliance with decree deemed to be desertion. *If the respondent shall fail to comply with a decree of the Court for restitution of conjugal rights such respondent shall thereupon be deemed to have been guilty of desertion without reasonable cause, and a suit for judicial separation may be forthwith instituted, and a sentence of judicial separation may be pronounced although the period of two years may have elapsed since the failure to comply with the decree for restitution of conjugal rights: and when any husband who has been guilty of desertion by failure on his part to comply with a decree for restitution of conjugal rights has also been guilty of adultery, the wife may forthwith present a petition for dissolution of her marriage, and the Court may pronounce a decree nisi for the dissolution of the marriage on the grounds of adultery coupled with desertion. Such decree nisi shall not be made absolute until after the expiration of six calendar months from the pronouncing thereof, unless the Court shall fix a shorter time.*

Note. See now Matrimonial Causes Act 1973, ss 1, 17 (pp 2471, 2479), replacing Divorce Reform Act 1969, ss 1, 2, 8 (pp 2319, 2322), replacing Matrimonial Causes Act 1965, ss 1(1), 12(1) (pp 2223, 2229), replacing Matrimonial Causes Act 1950, ss 1(1), 14(1) (pp 2120, 2125), replacing Supreme Court of Judicature (Consolidation) Act 1925, ss 176, 185(1) (pp 2054, 2058), as amended by Matrimonial Causes Act 1937, ss 2, 5. The right to claim restitution of conjugal rights was repealed by Matrimonial Proceedings and Property Act 1970, s 20 (p 2357).

6. Custody, &c. of children. *The Court may, at any time before final decree on any application for restitution of conjugal rights, or after final decree if the respondent shall fail to comply therewith, upon application for that purpose, make from time to time all such orders and provisions with respect to the custody, maintenance, and education of the children of the petitioner and respondent as might have been made by interim orders during the pendency of a trial for judicial separation between the same parties.*

Note. See now Matrimonial Causes Act 1973, ss 23, 42, 52(1) (pp 2484, 2518, 2525), replacing Matrimonial Proceedings and Property Act 1970, ss 3, 18, 19, 27(1) (pp 2346, 2356, 2359), replacing Matrimonial Causes Act 1965, ss 34(1), (4), 46(2) (pp 2242, 2249), replacing Matrimonial Causes Act 1950, s 26 (p 2131), replacing Supreme Court of Judicature (Consolidation) Act 1925, s 193 (p 2062), as extended by Matrimonial Causes Act 1937, s 10(4) (p 2092), and s 10(1) of that Act (p 2091).

7. (*Act to apply to England only.*)

MARRIED WOMEN'S PROPERTY ACT 1893

(56 & 57 Vict c 63)

An Act to amend the Married Women's Property Act 1882.   [5 December 1893]

1. Effect of contracts by married women. *Every contract hereafter entered into by a married woman, otherwise than as agent,*
  (*a*) *shall be deemed to be a contract entered into by her with respect to and to bind her separate property whether she is or is not in fact possessed of or entitled to any separate property at the time when she enters into such contract;*
  (*b*) *shall bind all separate property which she may at that time or thereafter be possessed of or entitled to; and*

(c)   shall also be enforceable by process of law against all property which she may thereafter while discovert be possessed of or entitled to;

Provided that nothing in this section contained shall render available to satisfy any liability or obligation arising out of such contract any separate property which at that time or thereafter she is restrained from anticipating.

2. Costs may be ordered to be paid out of property subject to restraint on anticipation. *In any action or proceeding now or hereafter instituted by a woman or by a next friend on her behalf, the court before which such action or proceeding is pending shall have jurisdiction by judgment or order from time to time to order payment of the costs of the opposite party out of property which is subject to a restraint on anticipation, and may enforce such payment by the appointment of a receiver and the sale of the property or otherwise as may be just.*

3. Will of married woman.   Section twenty-four of the Wills Act 1837, shall apply to the will of a married woman made during coverture whether she is or is not possessed of or entitled to any separate property at the time of making it, and such will shall not require to be re-executed or republished after the death of her husband.

4. Repeal.   *Subsections (3) and (4) of section one of the Married Women's Property Act 1882 are hereby repealed.*

5. Short title.   This Act may be cited as the Married Women's Property Act 1893.

6. Extent.   This Act shall not apply to Scotland.

Note.   Section 1 repealed by Law Reform (Married Women and Tortfeasors) Act 1935, ss 5(2), 8(2), Sch 2. Section 2 repealed by Married Women (Restraint Upon Anticipation) Act 1949, ss 1(4), 2(2), Sch 2. Section 4 repealed by Statute Law Revision Act 1908.

MATRIMONIAL CAUSES ACT 1907*

(7 Edw 7 c 12)

An Act to amend the Matrimonial Causes Act 1857 and 1866, by extending the powers of the Court in relation to Maintenance and Alimony, and leave to intervene.   [*9 August 1907*]

* This Act was repealed by Supreme Court of Judicature (Consolidation) Act 1925, Sch 6.

1. Power to grant maintenance and alimony [sic]—(*1*) *The Court may, if it thinks fit, on any decree for dissolution or nullity of marriage, order that the husband shall, to the satisfaction of the Court, secure to the wife such gross sum of money or such annual sum of money for any term not exceeding her life as, having regard to her fortune (if any), to the ability of the husband, and to the conduct of the parties, it may deem reasonable, and for that purpose may refer the matter to any one of the conveyancing counsel of the Court to settle and approve of a proper deed or instrument to be executed by all necessary parties, and the Court may, if it thinks fit, suspend the pronouncing of its decree until such deed shall have been duly executed.*

(*2*) *In any such case the Court may, if it thinks fit, make an order on the husband for payment to the wife during their joint lives of such monthly or weekly sum for her maintenance and support as the Court may think reasonable, and any such order may be made either in addition to or instead of an order under the last preceding subsection;*

Provided that—

(*a*)   *If the husband afterwards from any cause becomes unable to make such payments it shall be lawful for the Court to discharge or modify the order or temporarily to suspend the same as to the whole or any part of the money so ordered to be paid and again to revive the order wholly or in part as the Court may think fit; and*

(*b*)   *Where the Court has made any such order as is mentioned in this subsection and the Court is satisfied that the means of the husband have increased, the Court may, if it thinks fit, increase the amount payable under the order.*

(*3*) *Upon any petition for dissolution or nullity of marriage the Court shall have the same power to make interim orders for payment of money, by way of alimony or otherwise to the wife, as it has in a suit instituted for judicial separation.*

Note. See now Matrimonial Causes Act 1973, ss 22, 23, 31 (pp 2482, 2484, 2508), replacing Matri-monial Proceedings and Property Act 1970, ss 1, 2, 9 (pp 2345, 2350), replacing Matrimonial Causes Act 1965, ss 15, 16, 19, 31 (pp 2230, 2231, 2232, 2241), replacing Matrimonial Causes Act 1950, ss 19, 28 (pp 2128, 2132), replacing Supreme Court of Judicature (Consolidation) Act 1925, s 190 (p 2060), and Matrimonial Causes Act 1937, s 10 (p 2091).

2. Repeal of section 32 of 20 & 21 Vict c 85, and section 1 of 29 & 30 Vict c 32.
Section thirty-two of the Matrimonial Causes Act 1857, and section one of the Matrimonial Causes Act 1866, are hereby repealed.

Note. For Matrimonial Causes Act 1857, s 32, see p 2007.
For Matrimonial Causes Act 1866, s 1, see p 2022.

3. Power to allow intervention on terms. *In every case, not already provided for by law, in which any person is charged with adultery with any party to a suit, or in which the Court may consider, in the interest of any person not already a party to the suit, that such person should be made a party to the suit, the Court may, if it thinks fit, allow that person to intervene upon such terms (if any) as the Court may think just.*

Note. See now Matrimonial Causes Act 1973, s 49(5) (p 2523), replacing Matrimonial Causes Act 1965, s 44 (p 2249), replacing Matrimonial Causes Act 1950, s 31 (p 2133), replacing Supreme Court of Judicature (Consolidation) Act 1925, s 197 (p 2064).

4. Short title. *This Act may be cited as the Matrimonial Causes Act 1907, and may be cited with the Matrimonial Causes Acts 1857 to 1878.*

MAINTENANCE ORDERS (FACILITIES FOR ENFORCEMENT) ACT 1920*

(10 & 11 Geo 5 c 33)

An Act to facilitate the enforcement in England and Ireland† of Maintenance Orders made in other parts of His Majesty's Dominions and Protectorates‡ and vice versa.

[*16 August 1920*]

* This Act has been repealed by Maintenance Orders (Reciprocal Enforcement) Act 1972, s 22(2)(a), as from a day to be appointed (see note to s 49 of Act of 1972, p 2461). For provisions relating to maintenance orders registered in the High Court under Act of 1920 on the coming into force of s 1 of the Act of 1972, see s 23 of the Act of 1972 (p 2426).

1. Enforcement in England and Ireland† of maintenance orders made in His Majesty's dominions outside the United Kingdom—(*1*) *Where a maintenance order has, whether before or after the passing of this Act, been made against any person by any Court in any part of His Majesty's dominions outside the United Kingdom to which this Act extends, and a certified copy of the order has been transmitted by the governor of that part of His Majesty's dominions to the Secretary of State [Lord Chancellor], the Secretary of State [Lord Chancellor] shall send a copy of the order to the prescribed officer of a Court in England or Ireland† for registration; and on receipt thereof the order shall be registered in the prescribed manner, and shall, from the date of such registration, be of the same force and effect, and, subject to the provisions of this Act, all proceedings may be taken on such order as if it had been an order originally obtained in the Court in which it is so registered, and that Court shall have power to enforce the order accordingly.*

Note. Words 'Lord Chancellor' in square brackets substituted for words 'Secretary of State' by Transfer of Functions (Magistrates' Court and Family Law) Order 1992, SI 1992 No 709, art 4, as from 1 April 1992.

(*2*) *The Court in which an order is to be so registered as aforesaid shall, if the Court by which the order was made was a Court of superior jurisdiction, be the Probate, Divorce and Admiralty Division [Family Division] of the High Court, or in Ireland† the King's Bench*

Division (Matrimonial) of the High Court of Justice in Ireland, and, if the Court was not a Court of superior jurisdiction, be a Court of summary jurisdiction.

Note. Words in square brackets substituted for words 'Probate, Divorce and Admiralty Division' by Administration of Justice Act 1970, s 1(6)(a), Sch 2, para 2.

Appeals are governed by RSC Ord 56, r 5(2) (p 3908).

† The Act does *not* extend to the Republic of Ireland, and Orders made since the constitution of that State contain an express saving of the Irish Free State, when that was the appropriate designation for the Republic.

‡ The Maintenance Orders (Facilities for Enforcement) Order 1959 (SI 1959 No 377), as partially revoked by SI 1974 No 557, SI 1975 No 2188, SI 1979 No 116, SI 1983 No 1124 and amended by the Pakistan Act 1973, s 4(4), which now provides that this Act applies to the following countries and territories:

Antigua and Barbuda	Jamaica	St Vincent and the Grenadines
The Bahamas	Jersey	Seychelles
Belize	Kiribati	Sierra Leone
Botswana	Lesotho	Solomon Islands
Brunei	Malawi	Sri Lanka
Cayman Islands	Malaysia	Swaziland
Christmas Island	Mauritius	Trinidad and Tobago
Cocos (Keeling) Islands	Montserrat	Tuvalu
Cyprus	Newfoundland	Uganda
Dominica	Nigeria	Virgin Islands
The Gambia	Prince Edward Island	Yukon Territory
Grenada	St Kitts and Nevis	Zambia
Guernsey	St Lucia	Zanzibar*
Guyana		

* Ie that part of the United Republic of Tanzania to which the 1972 Act does not apply

2. Transmission of maintenance orders made in England or Ireland. *Where a Court in England or Ireland* has, whether before or after the commencement of this Act, made a maintenance order against any person, and it is proved to that Court that the person against whom the order was made is resident in some part of His Majesty's dominions outside the United Kingdom to which this Act extends,† the Court shall send to the Secretary of State [Lord Chancellor] for transmission to the governor of that part of His Majesty's dominions a certified copy of the order.*

Note. Words 'Lord Chancellor' in square brackets substituted for words 'Secretary of State' by virtue of Transfer of Functions (Magistrates' Courts and Family Law) Order 1992, SI 1992 No 709, art 4, as from 1 April 1992.

3. Power to make provisional orders of maintenance against persons resident in His Majesty's dominions outside the United Kingdom—*(1) Where an application is made to a court of summary jurisdiction in England or Ireland* for a maintenance order against any person, and it is proved that that person is resident in a part of His Majesty's dominions outside the United Kingdom to which this Act extends,† the Court may, in the absence of that person, if after hearing the evidence it is satisfied of the justice of the application, make any such order as it might have made if a summons had been duly served on that person and he [that person had been resident in England and Wales, had received reasonable notice of the date of the hearing of the application and] had failed to appear at the hearing, but in such case the order shall be provisional only, and shall have no effect unless and until confirmed by a competent Court in such part of His Majesty's dominions as aforesaid.*

(2) The evidence of any witness who is examined on any such application shall be put into writing, and such deposition shall be read over to and signed by him.

Note. Words in square brackets substituted for words 'a summons had been duly served on that person and he' by Maintenance Orders (Reciprocal Enforcement Act 1992, s 1(1), Sch 1, Part I, para 1(2), as from 5 April 1993.

(3) Where such an order is made, the Court shall send to the Secretary of State [Lord Chancellor] for transmission to the governor of the part of His Majesty's dominions in which

the persons against whom the order is made is alleged to reside the depositions so taken and a certified copy of the order, together with a statement of the grounds on which the making of the order might have been opposed if the person against whom the order is made had been duly served with a summons [*resident in England and Wales, had received reasonable notice of the date of the hearing*] and had appeared at the hearing, and such information as the Court possesses for facilitating the identification of that person, and ascertaining his whereabouts.

Note. Words 'Lord Chancellor' in square brackets substituted for words 'Secretary of State' by virtue of Transfer of Functions (Magistrates' Courts and Family Law) Order 1992, SI 1992 No 709, art 4, as from 1 April 1992. Words in second pair of square brackets substituted for words 'duly served with a summons' by Maintenance Orders (Reciprocal Enforcement) Act 1992, s 1(1), Sch 1, Part I, para 1(3), as from 5 April 1993.

* See note † above.
† See note ‡ above.

(*4*) *Where any such provisional order has come before a Court in a part of His Majesty's dominions outside the United Kingdom to which this Act extends for confirmation, and the order has by that Court been remitted to the court of summary jurisdiction which made the order for the purpose of taking further evidence that Court or any other court of summary jurisdiction sitting and acting for the same place* [*appointed for the same commission area* (*within the meaning of section 1 of the Administration of Justice Act 1973* [*the Justices of the Peace Act 1979*])] *shall, after giving the prescribed notice, proceed to take evidence in like manner and subject to the like conditions as the evidence in support of the original application.*

If upon the hearing of such evidence it appears to the Court that the order ought not to have been made, the Court may rescind [*revoke*] *the order, but in any other case the depositions shall be sent to the Secretary of State* [*Lord Chancellor*] *and dealt with in like manner as the original depositions.*

Note. Words in first pair of square brackets substituted for 'sitting and acting for the same place' by Domestic Proceedings and Magistrates' Courts Act 1978, s 89, Sch 2, para 2, as from 1 February 1981, and reference to Justices of the Peace Act 1979 substituted for reference to Act of 1973 by Act of 1979, s 71, Sch 2, para 1, as from the same date. Word 'revoke' substituted for word 'rescind' by Maintenance Orders (Reciprocal Enforcement) Act 1992, s 1, Sch 1, Part I, para 1, as from 5 April 1993. Words 'Lord Chancellor' in square brackets substituted for words 'Secretary of State' by virtue of Transfer of Functions (Magistrates' Courts and Family Law) Order 1992, SI 1992 No 709, art 4, as from 1 April 1992.

(*5*) *The confirmation of an order made under this section shall not affect any power of a court of summary jurisdiction to vary or rescind* [*revoke*] *that order: Provided that on the making of a varying or rescinding* [*revoking*] *order the Court shall send a certified copy thereof to the Secretary of State* [*Lord Chancellor*] *for transmission to the governor of the part of His Majesty's dominions in which the original order was confirmed, and that in the case of an order varying the original order the order shall not have any effect unless and until confirmed in like manner as the original order.*

Note. Words 'revoke' and 'revoking' in square brackets substituted for words 'rescind' and 'rescinding' respectively by Maintenance Orders (Reciprocal Enforcement) Act 1992, s 1(1), Sch 1, Part I, para 1(5), as from 5 April 1993. Words 'Lord Chancellor' in square brackets substituted for words 'Secretary of State' by virtue of Transfer of Functions (Magistrates' Courts and Family Law) Order 1992, SI 1992 No 709, art 4, as from 1 April 1992.

(*6*) *The applicant shall have the same right of appeal, if any, against a refusal to make a provisional order as he would have had against a refusal to make the order had a summons been duly served on the person against whom the order is sought to be made* [*the person against whom the order is sought to be made been resident in England and Wales and received reasonable notice of the date of the hearing of the application*].

Note. Words in square brackets substituted for words 'a summons' to the end by Maintenance Orders (Reciprocal Enforcement) Act 1992, s 1(1), Sch 1, Part I, para 1(6), as from 5 April 1993.

[(*7*) *Where subsection* (*1*) *of section 60 of the Magistrates' Courts Act 1980* (*revocation, variation etc of orders for periodical payment*) *applies in relation to an order made under this* section which has been confirmed, that subsection shall have effect as if for the words 'by order on complaint,' there were substituted 'on an application being made, by order'.

(*8*) *In this section 'revoke' includes discharge.*]

Note. Sub-ss (7), (8) added by Maintenance Orders (Reciprocal Enforcement) Act 1992, s 1, Sch 1, Part I, para 1, as from 5 April 1993.

4. Power of court of summary jurisdiction to confirm maintenance order made out of the United Kingdom—(*1*) *Where a maintenance order has been made by a Court in a part of His Majesty's dominions outside the United Kingdom to which this Act extends,* and the order is provisional only and has no effect unless and until confirmed by a court of summary jurisdiction in England or Ireland, and a certified copy of the order, together with the depositions of witnesses and a statement of the grounds on which the order might have been opposed has been transmitted to the Secretary of State [Lord Chancellor], and it appears to the Secretary of State [Lord Chancellor] that the person against whom the order was made is resident in England or Ireland, the Secretary of State [Lord Chancellor] may send the said documents to the prescribed officer of a court of summary jurisdiction, with a requisition that a summons be issued calling upon the person [notice be served on the person informing him that he may attend a hearing at the time and place specified in the notice] to show cause why that order should not be confirmed, and upon receipt of such documents and requisition the Court shall issue such a summons and cause it to be served upon such person.*

Note. Words 'Lord Chancellor' in square brackets substituted for words 'Secretary of State' by virtue of Transfer of Functions (Magistrates' Courts and Family Law) Order 1992, SI 1992 No 709, art 4, as from 1 April 1992. Other words in square brackets substituted for words 'summons be issued calling upon the person' and 'issue such a summons and cause it' respectively, by Maintenance Orders (Reciprocal Enforcement) Act 1992, s 1(1), Sch 1, Part I, para 2(2), as from 5 April 1993.

(*2*) *A summons so issued may be served in England or Ireland in the same manner as if it had been originally issued or subsequently endorsed by a court of summary jurisdiction having jurisdiction in the place where the person happens to be.*

[(*2*) *A notice required to be served under this section may be served by post.*]

Note. Sub-s (2) in square brackets substituted by Maintenance Orders (Reciprocal Enforcement) Act 1992, s 1(1), Sch 1, Part I, para 2(3), as from 5 April 1993.

(*3*) *At the hearing it shall be open to the person on whom the summons [notice] was served to raise any defence which he might have raised in the original proceedings had he been a party thereto, but no other defence [oppose the confirmation of the order on any grounds on which he might have opposed the making of the order in the original proceedings had he been a party to them, but on no other grounds], and the certificate from the Court which made the provisional order stating the grounds on which the making of the order might have been opposed if the person against whom the order was made had been a party to the proceedings shall be conclusive evidence that those grounds are grounds on which objection may be taken.*

Note. Words in square brackets substituted for words 'notice' and words from 'raise any defence' to 'no other defence' respectively, by Maintenance Orders (Reciprocal Enforcement) Act 1992, s 1(1), Sch 1, Part I, para 2(4), as from 5 April 1993.

(*4*) *If at the hearing the person served with the summons [notice] does not appear or, on appearing, fails to satisfy the Court that the order ought not to be confirmed, the Court may confirm the order either without modification or with such modifications as to the Court after hearing the evidence may seem just.*

Note. Word in square brackets substituted for word 'summons' by Maintenance Orders (Reciprocal Enforcement) Act 1992, s 1(1), Sch 1, Part I, para 2(5), as from 5 April 1993.

(*5*) *If the person against whom the summons was issued [served with the notice] appears at the hearing and satisfies the Court that for the purpose of any defence [establishing any grounds on which he opposes the confirmation of the order] it is necessary to remit the case to*

---

* See note on p 2036, for places to which the Act extends.

the Court which made the provisional order for the taking of any further evidence, the Court may so remit the case and adjourn the proceedings for the purpose.

Note. Words in square brackets substituted for words 'against whom the summons was issued' and 'any defence' respectively, by Maintenance Orders (Reciprocal Enforcement) Act 1992, s 1(1), Sch 1, Part I, para 2(6), as from 5 April 1993.

[(*5A*) *Where a magistrates' court confirms a provisional order under this section, it shall at the same time exercise one of its powers under subsection (5B).*

(*5B*) *The powers of the court are—*

(*a*) *the power to order that payments under the order be made directly to the clerk of the court or the clerk of any other magistrates' court;*

(*b*) *the power to order that payments under the order be made to the clerk of the court, or to the clerk of any other magistrates' court, by such method of payment falling within section 59(6) of the Magistrates' Courts Act 1980 (standing order, etc) as may be specified;*

(*c*) *the power to make an attachment of earnings order under the Attachment of Earnings Act 1971 to secure payments under the order.*

(*5C*) *In deciding which of the powers under subsection (5B) it is to exercise, the court shall have regard to any representations made by the person liable to make payments under the order.*

(*5D*) *Subsection (4) of section 59 of the Magistrates' Courts Act 1980 (power of court to require debtor to open account) shall apply for the purposes of subsection (5B) as it applies for the purposes of that section but as if for paragraph (a) there were substituted—*

'(*a*) *the court proposes to exercise its power under paragraph (b) of section 4(5B) of the Maintenance Orders (Facilities for Enforcement) Act 1920, and'.*]

Note. Sub-ss (5A)–(5D) in square brackets inserted by Maintenance Enforcement Act 1991, s 10, Sch 1, para 1(1), as from 1 April 1992.

(*6*) *Where a provisional order has been confirmed under this section, it may be varied or rescinded in like manner as if it had originally been made by the confirming Court, and where on an application for rescission or variation the Court is satisfied that it is necessary to remit the case to the Court which made the order for the purpose of taking any further evidence, the Court may so remit the case and adjourn the proceedings for the purpose.*

[(*6*) *Subject to subsection (6A), where a provisional order has been confirmed under this section, it may be varied or revoked in like manner as if it had originally been made by the confirming court.*

(*6A*) *Where the confirming court is a magistrates' court, section 60 of the Magistrates' Courts Act 1980 (revocation, variation etc of orders for periodical payment) shall have effect in relation to a provisional order confirmed under this section—*

(*za*) *as if in subsection (1) for the words 'by order on complaint' there were substituted 'on an application being made, by order'*]

(*a*) *as if in subsection (3) for the words 'paragraphs (a) to (d) of section 59(3) above' there were substituted 'section 4(5B) of the Maintenance Orders (Facilities for Enforcement) Act 1920';*

(*b*) *as if in subsection (4) for paragraph (b) there were substituted—*

'(*b*) *payments under the order are required to be made to the clerk of the court, or to the clerk of any other magistrates' court, by any method of payment falling within section 59(6) above (standing order, etc)';*

and as if after the words 'the court' there were inserted 'which made the order';

(*c*) *as if in subsection (5) for the words 'to the clerk' there were substituted 'in accordance with paragraph (a) of section 4(5B) of the Maintenance Orders (Facilities for Enforcement) Act 1920';*

(*d*) *as if in subsection (7), paragraph (c) and the word 'and' immediately preceding it were omitted;*

(*e*) *as if in subsection (8) for the words 'paragraphs (a) to (d) of section 59(3) above' there were substituted 'section 4(5B) of the Maintenance Orders (Facilities for Enforcement) Act 1920';*

(*f*) *as if for subsections (9) and (10) there were substituted the following subsections—*

'(9) *In deciding, for the purposes of subsections (3) and (8) above, which of the powers under section 4(5B) of the Maintenance Orders (Facilities for Enforcement) Act 1920 it is to exercise, the court shall have regard to any representations made by the debtor.*

(10) *Subsection (4) of section 59 above (power of court to require debtor to open account) shall apply for the purposes of subsections (3) and (8) above as it applies for the purposes of that section but as if for paragraph (a) there were substituted—*

"(a) *the court proposes to exercise its power under paragraph (b) of section 4(5B) of the Maintenance Orders (Facilities for Enforcement) Act 1920, and".'*

Note. Sub-s (6A)(za) inserted by Maintenance Orders (Reciprocal Enforcement) Act 1992, s 1(1), Sch 1, Part I, para 2(7), as from 5 April 1993.

(6B) *Where on an application for variation or revocation the confirming court is satisfied that it is necessary to remit the case to the court which made the order for the purpose of taking any further evidence, the court may so remit the case and adjourn the proceedings for the purpose.*]

Note. Sub-ss (6), (6A), (6B) in square brackets substituted for original sub-s (6) by Maintenance Enforcement Act 1991, s 10, Sch 1, para 1(2), as from 1 April 1992.

(7) *Where an order has been so confirmed, the person bound thereby shall have the same right of appeal, if any, against the confirmation of the order as he would have had against the making of the order had the order been an order made by the Court confirming the order.*

[**4A. Variation and revocation of maintenance orders**—(1) *This section applies to—*

(a) *any maintenance order made by virtue of section 3 of this Act which has been confirmed as mentioned in that section; and*

(b) *any maintenance order which has been confirmed under section 4 of this Act.*

(2) *Where the respondent to an application for the variation or revocation of a maintenance order to which this section applies is residing in a part of Her Majesty's dominions outside the United Kingdom to which this Act extends, a magistrates' court in England and Wales shall have jurisdiction to hear the application (where it would not have such jurisdiction apart from this subsection) if that court would have had jurisdiction to hear it had the respondent been residing in England and Wales.*

(3) *Where the defendant to a complaint [respondent to an application] for the variation or revocation of a maintenance order to which this section applies is residing in a part of Her Majesty's dominions outside the United Kingdom to which this Act extends, a court of summary jurisdiction in Northern Ireland shall have jurisdiction to hear the complaint [the application (where it would not have such jurisdiction apart from this subsection)] if that court would have had jurisdiction to hear it had the defendant [respondent] been residing in Northern Ireland.*

(4) *Where—*

(a) *the respondent to an application for the variation or revocation of a maintenance order to which this section applies does not appear at the time and place appointed for the hearing of the application by a magistrates' court in England and Wales, and*

(b) *the court is satisfied that the respondent is residing in a part of Her Majesty's dominions outside the United Kingdom to which this Act extends,*

the court may proceed to hear and determine the application at the time and place appointed for the hearing or for any adjourned hearing in like manner as if the respondent had appeared at that time and place.

(5) *Subsection (4) shall apply to Northern Ireland with the following modifications—*

(a) *for the word 'respondent' (in each place where it occurs) there shall be substituted 'defendant',*

(b) *for the words 'an application' and 'the application' (in each place where they occur) there shall be substituted 'a complaint' and 'the complaint' respectively, and* (*c*) for the words 'a magistrates' court in England and Wales' there shall be substituted 'a court of summary jurisdiction in Northern Ireland'.

(*6*) In this section 'revocation' includes discharge.]

Note. This section inserted by Maintenance Orders (Reciprocal Enforcement) Act 1992, s 1, Sch 1, Part I, para 3, as from 5 April 1993. In sub-s (3) words in square brackets substituted for words 'defendant to a complaint', 'the complaint' and 'defendant', and sub-s (5)(a), (b) repealed, by Children (Northern Ireland) Order 1995, SI 1995 No 755, art 185, Sch 9, para 5, Sch 10, as from 4 November 1996.

5. Power of Secretary of State to make regulations for facilitating communications between Courts. *The Secretary of State [Lord Chancellor] may make regulations as to the manner in which a case can be remitted by a Court authorised to confirm a provisional order to the Court which made the provisional order, and generally for facilitating communications between such Courts.*

Note. Words 'Lord Chancellor' in square brackets substituted for words 'Secretary of State' by virtue of Transfer of Functions (Magistrates' Courts and Family Law) Order 1992, SI 1992 No 709, art 4, as from 1 April 1992.

6. Mode of enforcing orders—(*1*) *A court of summary jurisdiction in which an order has been registered under this Act or by which an order has been confirmed under this Act, and the officers of such Court, shall take all such steps for enforcing the order as may be prescribed.*

(*2*) *Every such order shall be enforceable in like manner as if the order were for the payment of a civil debt recoverable summarily:*

Provided that, if the order is of such a nature that if made by the Court in which it is so registered, or by which it is so confirmed, it would be enforceable in like manner as an order of affiliation [as a magistrates' court maintenance order], the order shall be so enforceable [the order shall, subject to the modifications of sections 76 and 93 of the Magistrates' Courts Act 1980 (enforcement of sums adjudged to be paid and complaint for arrears) specified in subsections (2ZA) and (2ZB) of section 18 of the Maintenance Orders Act 1950 (enforcement of registered orders), be so enforceable].

[In this subsection 'magistrates' court maintenance order' has the same meaning as in section 150(1) of the Magistrates' Courts Act 1980.]

(*3*) *A warrant of distress or commitment issued by a court of summary jurisdiction for the purpose of enforcing any order so registered or confirmed may be executed in any part of the United Kingdom in the same manner as if the warrant had been originally issued or subsequently endorsed by a court of summary jurisdiction having jurisdiction in the place where the warrant is executed.*

Note. First set of words in square brackets substituted for words 'in like manner as an order of affiliation' and third set of words inserted by Family Law Reform Act 1987, s 33(1), Sch 2, para 1, as from 1 April 1989; second set of words in square brackets substituted for words 'the order shall be so enforceable' by Maintenance Enforcement Act 1991, s 9, Sch 1, para 2, as from 1 April 1992.

7. Application of Summary Jurisdiction Acts[—(*1*)] *The Summary Jurisdiction Acts shall apply to proceedings before courts of summary jurisdiction under this Act in like manner as they apply to proceedings under those Acts, and the power of the Lord Chancellor to make rules under section twenty-nine of the Summary Jurisdiction Act 1879, shall include power to make rules regulating the procedure of courts of summary jurisdiction under this Act.*

[(*2*) *Without prejudice to the generality of the power to make rules under section 144 of the Magistrates' Courts Act 1980 (magistrates' courts rules), for the purpose of giving effect to this Act such rules may make, in relation to any proceedings brought under or by virtue of this Act, any provision which*—

(*a*) *falls within subsection (2) of section 93 of the Children Act 1989, and*

(*b*) *may be made in relation to relevant proceedings under that section.*]

Note. Sub-s (1) numbered as such, and sub-s (2) added, by Maintenance Orders (Reciprocal Enforcement) Act 1992, s 1, Sch 1, Part I, para 4, as from 5 April 1993. In sub-s (1) words from 'and the power' to end of the sub-section repealed by Justices of the Peace Act 1949, s 46(2), Seventh Schedule, Part II.

See Maintenance Orders (Facilities for Enforcement) Rules 1922 (SR & O 1922, No 1355): Maintenance Orders Act 1950 (p 2134), and Maintenance Orders Act 1958 (p 2190).

8. Proof of documents signed by officers of Court. *Any document purporting to be signed by a judge or officer of a Court outside the United Kingdom shall, until the contrary is proved, be deemed to have been so signed without proof of the signature or judicial or official character of the person appearing to have signed it, and the officer of a Court by whom a document is signed shall, until the contrary is proved, be deemed to have been the proper officer of the Court to sign the document.*

9. Depositions to be evidence. *Depositions taken in a Court in a part of His Majesty's dominions outside the United Kingdom to which this Act extends* for the purposes of this Act, may be received in evidence in proceedings before courts of summary jurisdiction under this Act.*

* See note on p 2036, for places to which the Act extends. The Act does not extend to the Republic of Ireland.

10. Interpretation. *For the purposes of this Act, the expression 'maintenance order' means an order other than an order of affiliation for the periodical payment of sums of money towards the maintenance of the wife or other dependants of the person against whom the order is made, and the expression 'dependants' means such persons as that person is, according to the law in force in the part of His Majesty's dominions in which the maintenance order was made, liable to maintain; the expression 'certified copy' in relation to an order of a Court means a copy of the order certified by the proper officer of the Court to be a true copy, and the expression 'prescribed' means prescribed by rules of Court.*

11. Application to Ireland. *In the application of this Act to Ireland the following modifications shall be made:*

[(*za*) *In section 3(1), (3) and (6) for the words 'England and Wales' there shall be substituted the words 'Northern Ireland' and for subsection (7) of that section there shall be substituted the following subsection—*

'(7) *Where paragraph (1) of Article 86 of the Magistrates' Courts (Northern Ireland) Order 1981 (revocation, variation, etc, of orders for periodical payment) applies in relation to an order made under this section which has been confirmed, that paragraph shall have effect as if for the words "by order on complaint" there were substituted the words "on an application being made, by order".';]*

Note. Para (za) inserted by Children (Northern Ireland) Order 1995, SI 1995 No 755, art 185, Sch 9, para 6, Sch 10, as from 4 November 1996.

(*a*) *The Lord Chancellor of Ireland may make rules regulating the procedure of courts of summary jurisdiction under this Act, and other matters incidental thereto:*

Note. See Maintenance Orders (Facilities for Enforcement) Rules (Northern Ireland) 1925, SR & O 1925 No 254).

(*b*) *Orders intended to be registered or confirmed in Ireland shall be transmitted by the Secretary of State [Lord Chancellor] to the prescribed officer of a Court in Ireland through the Lord Chancellor of Ireland:*

Note. Words 'Lord Chancellor' in square brackets substituted for words 'Secretary of State' by virtue of Transfer of Functions (Magistrates' Courts and Family Law) Order 1992, SI 1992 No 709, art 4, as from 1 April 1992.

(*c*) *The expression 'maintenance order' includes an order or decree for the recovery or repayment of the cost of relief or maintenance made by virtue of the provisions of the Poor Relief (Ireland) Acts 1839 to 1914.*

[(*a*) *In section 4 (power of court of summary jurisdiction to confirm maintenance order made out of UK) after subsection (5) there shall be inserted the following subsections—*

'(5A) *Where a court of summary jurisdiction confirms a provisional order under this section, it shall at the same time exercise one of its powers under subsection (5B).*

(5B) *The powers of the court are—*

(a) *the power to order that payments under the order be made directly to the collecting officer;*

   (*b*) the power to order that payments under the order be made to the collecting officer by such method of payment falling within Article 85(7) of the Magistrates' Courts (*Northern Ireland*) Order 1981 (*standing order, etc*) as may be specified;

   (*c*) the power to make an attachment of earnings order under Part IX of the Order of 1981 to secure payments under the order;

and in this subsection "collecting officer" means the officer mentioned in Article 85(4) of the Order of 1981.

(*5C*) In deciding which of the powers under subsection (*5B*) it is to exercise, the court shall have regard to any representations made by the person liable to make payments under the order.

(*5D*) Paragraph (*5*) of Article 85 of the Magistrates' Courts (*Northern Ireland*) Order 1981 (*power of court to require debtor to open account*) shall apply for the purposes of subsection (*5B*) as it applies for the purposes of that Article but as if for sub-paragraph (*a*) there were substituted—

   "(*a*) the court proposes to exercise its power under paragraph (*b*) of section 4(*5B*) of the Maintenance Orders (*Facilities for Enforcement*) Act 1920, and";'

(*b*) In section 4, for subsection (6) there shall be substituted the following subsections—

'(*6*) Subject to subsection (*6A*), where a provisional order has been confirmed under this section, it may be varied or revoked in like manner as if it had originally been made by the confirming court.

(*6A*) Where the confirming court is a court of summary jurisdiction, Article 86 of the Magistrates' Courts (*Northern Ireland*) Order 1981 (*revocation, variation, etc, of orders for periodical payment*) shall have effect in relation to a provisional order confirmed under this section—

   [(*za*) as if in paragraph (*1*) for the words "by order on complaint" there were substituted "on an application being made, by order";]

   (*a*) as if in paragraph (*3*) for the words "sub-paragraphs (*a*) to (*d*) of Article 85(*3*)" there were substituted "section 4(*5B*) of the Maintenance Orders (*Facilities for Enforcement*) Act 1920";

   (*b*) as if in paragraph (*4*) for sub-paragraph (*b*) there were substituted—

     "(*b*) payments under the order are required to be made to the collecting officer by any method of payment falling within Article 85(7) (*standing order, etc*)"; and as if after the words "petty sessions" there were inserted "for the petty sessions district for which the court which made the order acts";

   (*c*) as if in paragraph (*5*) for the words "to the collecting officer" there were substituted "in accordance with paragraph (*a*) of section 4(*5B*) of the Maintenance Orders (*Facilities for Enforcement*) Act 1920";

   (*d*) as if in paragraph (*7*), sub-paragraph (*c*) and the word "and" immediately preceding it were omitted;

   (*e*) as if in paragraph (*8*) for the words "sub-paragraphs (*a*) to (*d*) of Article 85(*3*)" there were substituted "section 4(*5B*) of the Maintenance Orders (*Facilities for Enforcement*) Act 1920";

   (*f*) as if for paragraphs (*9*) and (*10*) there were substituted the following paragraphs—

     "(*9*) In deciding, for the purposes of paragraphs (*3*) and (*8*), which of the powers under section 4(*5B*) of the Maintenance Orders (*Facilities for Enforcement*) Act 1920 it is to exercise, the court shall have regard to any representations made by the debtor.

     (*10*) Paragraph (*5*) of Article 85 (*power of court to require debtor to open account*) shall apply for the purposes of paragraphs (*3*) and (*8*) as it applies for the purposes of that Article but as if for sub-paragraph (*a*) there were substituted—

       '(*a*) the court proposes to exercise its power under paragraph (*b*) of section 4(*5B*) of the Maintenance Orders (*Facilities for Enforcement*) Act 1920, and'."

(*6B*) *Where on an application for variation or revocation the confirming court is satisfied that it is necessary to remit the case to the court which made the order for the purpose of taking any further evidence, the court may so remit the case and adjourn the proceedings for the purpose.';*

(*c*) *In section 6 (mode of enforcing orders registered or confirmed by courts under Act) in subsection (2) for the words 'the order shall be so enforceable' there shall be substituted 'the order shall, subject to the modifications of Article 98 of the Magistrates' Courts (Northern Ireland) Order 1981 (enforcement of sums adjudged to be paid and complaint for arrears) specified in subsection (3ZA) of section 18 of the Maintenance Orders Act 1950 (enforcement of registered orders), be so enforceable'.*]

[(*c*) *In section 6 (mode of enforcing orders), in the proviso to subsection (2), for the words from 'in like manner' to the end substitute 'as an order to which Article 98 of the Magistrates' Courts (Northern Ireland) Order 1981 applies, the order shall be so enforceable subject to the modifications of that Article specified in subsection (3ZA) of section 18 of the Maintenance Orders Act 1950 (enforcement of registered orders)';*

(*cc*) *In section 7 (application of Summary Jurisdiction Acts), after subsection (2) there shall be added the following subsection—*

'(*3*) *Without prejudice to the generality of the power to make rules under Article 13 of the Magistrates' Courts (Northern Ireland) Order 1981 (magistrates' courts rules), for the purpose of giving effect to this Act such rules may make, in relation to any proceedings brought under or by virtue of this Act, any provision which—*

(*a*) *falls within paragraph (2) of Article 165 of the Children (Northern Ireland) Order 1995, and*

(*b*) *may be made in relation to relevant proceedings under that Article'.*]

Note. Paras (a)–(c) in square brackets substituted for original paras (a)–(c) by Family Law (Northern Ireland) Order 1993, SI 1993 No 1576, art 11, Sch 1, para 1, as from 4 November 1996. Para (b) amended, and para (c) further substituted by subsequent paras (c), (cc) in square brackets, by Children (Northern Ireland) Order 1995, SI 1995 No 755, art 185, Sch 9, para 6, Sch 10, as from 4 November 1996.

[(*d*) *the amendments of section 3(1), (3) and (6) and section 4 made by the Maintenance Orders (Reciprocal Enforcement) Act 1992 shall be disregarded.*]

Note. Para (d) added by Maintenance Orders (Reciprocal Enforcement) Act 1992, s 1, Sch 1, Part I, para 5, as from 5 April 1993. Para (d) repealed by Children (Northern Ireland) Order 1995, SI 1995 No 755, art 185, Sch 9, para 6, Sch 10, as from a day to be appointed.

12. Extent of Act—(*1*) *Where His Majesty is satisfied that reciprocal provisions have been made by the legislature of any part of His Majesty's dominions outside the United Kingdom for the enforcement within that part of maintenance orders made by Courts within England and Ireland, His Majesty may by Order in Council extend this Act to that part, and thereupon that part shall become a part of His Majesty's dominions to which this Act extends.**

(*2*) *His Majesty may by Order in Council extend this Act to any British protectorate, and where so extended this Act shall apply as if any such protectorate was a part of His Majesty's dominions to which this Act extends.*

Note. For power to revoke or vary an Order in Council made under this section, see Maintenance Orders Act 1958, s 19 (p 2201).

13. *This Act may be cited as the Maintenance Orders (Facilities for Enforcement) Act 1920.*

Note. See also Maintenance Orders Act 1950 (p 2134) and Maintenance Orders Act 1958 (p 2170), which deal with position within the United Kingdom.

MARRIED WOMEN (MAINTENANCE) ACT 1920*

(10 & 11 Geo 5 c 63)

An Act to provide for the inclusion in Orders made under the Summary Jurisdiction (Married Women) Act 1895, of a provision for the Maintenance of the Children of the Marriage under sixteen.   [*23 December 1920*]

* Whole Act repealed by Matrimonial Proceedings (Magistrates' Courts) Act 1960, s 18(1), Schedule.

1. Provision for maintenance of children—(*1*) *An order under section four of the Summary Jurisdiction (Married Women) Act 1895, whether as originally enacted or as extended by section five of the Licensing Act 1902, made on the application of a married woman, which contains a provision committing the legal custody of any children of the marriage to the applicant, may, in addition to any other provision authorised by the Act, include a provision that the husband shall pay to the applicant, or to any officer of the Court or third person on her behalf, a weekly sum not exceeding ten shillings for the maintenance of each such child until such child attains the age of sixteen years.*

(*2*) *Any such order made before the passing of this Act may be varied, on the application of the married woman, so as to include from the date of the variation of the order such a provision for the maintenance of the children as aforesaid.*

2. Short title. *This Act may be cited as the Married Women (Maintenance) Act, 1920, and the Summary Jurisdiction (Married Women) Act 1895, and this Act may be cited together as the Married Women (Maintenance) Acts 1895 and 1920.*

ADMINISTRATION OF JUSTICE ACT 1920

(10 & 11 Geo 5 c 81)

An Act to amend the law with respect to the administration of justice and with respect to the constitution of the Supreme Court, to facilitate the reciprocal enforcement of judgments and awards in the United Kingdom and other parts of His Majesty's Dominions or Territories under His Majesty's protection, and to regulate the fees chargeable by, and on the registration of, Commissioners for Oaths.

[23 December 1920]

*   *   *   *   *

PART II

RECIPROCAL ENFORCEMENT OF JUDGMENTS IN THE UNITED KINGDOM AND IN OTHER PARTS OF HIS MAJESTY'S DOMINIONS†

9. Enforcement in the United Kingdom of judgments obtained in superior courts in other British dominions—(1) Where a judgment has been obtained in a superior court in any part of His Majesty's dominions outside the United Kingdom to which this Part of this Act extends,† the judgment creditor may apply to the High

---

† See Reciprocal Enforcement of Judgments (Administration of Justice Act 1920, Part II) (Consolidation) Order 1984, SI 1984 No 129, as amended by SI 1985 No 1994, extending this Part of this Act to the following countries and territories: Anguilla, Antigua and Barbuda, Bahamas, Barbados, Belize, Bermuda, Botswana, British Indian Ocean Territory, Cayman Islands, Christmas Island, Cocos (Keeling) Islands, Republic of Cyprus, Dominica, Falkland Islands, Fiji, The Gambia, Ghana, Gibraltar, Grenada, Guyana, Hong Kong, Jamaica, Kenya, Kiribati, Lesotho, Malawi, Malaysia, Malta, Mauritius, Montserrat, Newfoundland, New South Wales, New Zealand, Nigeria, Territory of Norfolk Island, Northern Territory of Australia, Papua New Guinea, Queensland, St Christopher and Nevis, St Helena, St Lucia, St Vincent and the Grenadines, Saskatchewan, Seychelles, Sierra Leone, Singapore, Solomon Islands, South Australia, Sovereign Base Areas of Akrotiri and Dhekelia in Cyprus, Sri Lanka, Swaziland, Tanzania, Tasmania, Trinidad and Tobago, Turks and Caicos Islands, Tuvalu, Uganda, Victoria, Western Australia, Zambia, Zimbabwe.

By Order in Council made under s 7(1) of the Foreign Judgments (Reciprocal Enforcement) Act 1933 (SR & O 1933, No 1073), no further colonies or dominions are to be included under the arrangement for reciprocal enforcement provided for in the 1920 Act, other than those territories to which the Act was extended before 10 November 1933. Moreover, if, at any time, any one of these territories is brought within the provisions of the Act of 1933, then the Act of 1920 will cease to apply to it (s 7(2) of the Act of 1933, p 2082). For procedure, see RSC, Ord 71 (p 3956).

Court in England or Ireland,† or to the Court of Session in Scotland, at any time within twelve months after the date of the judgment, or such longer period as may be allowed by the Court, to have the judgment registered in the Court, and on any such application the Court may, if in all the circumstances of the case they think it is just and convenient that the judgment should be enforced in the United Kingdom, and subject to the provisions of this section, order the judgment to be registered accordingly.

(2) No judgment shall be ordered to be registered under this section if—

(a) the original Court acted without jurisdiction; or

(b) the judgment debtor, being a person who was neither carrying on business nor ordinarily resident within the jurisdiction of the original Court, did not voluntarily appear or otherwise submit or agree to submit to the jurisdiction of that Court; or

(c) the judgment debtor, being the defendant in the proceedings, was not duly served with the process of the original Court and did not appear, notwithstanding that he was ordinarily resident or was carrying on business within the jurisdiction of that Court or agreed to submit to the jurisdiction of that Court; or

(d) the judgment was obtained by fraud; or

(e) the judgment debtor satisfies the registering Court either that an appeal is pending, or that he is entitled and intends to appeal, against the judgment; or

(f) the judgment was in respect of a cause of action which for reasons of public policy or for some other similar reason could not have been entertained by the registering Court.

(3) Where a judgment is registered under this section—

(a) the judgment shall, as from the date of registration, be of the same force and effect, and proceedings may be taken thereon, as if it had been a judgment originally obtained or entered upon the date of registration in the registering Court;

Note. See Administration of Justice Act 1956, s 40(b) (p 2172), for effect of Debtors Act 1869, s 5.

(b) the registering Court shall have the same control and jurisdiction over the judgment as it has over similar judgments given by itself, but in so far only as relates to execution under this section;

(c) the reasonable costs of and incidental to the registration of the judgment (including the costs of obtaining a certified copy thereof from the original Court and of the application for registration) shall be recoverable in like manner as if they were sums payable under the judgment.

(4) Rules of Court shall provide—

(a) for service on the judgment debtor of notice of the registration of a judgment under this section; and

(b) for enabling the registering Court on an application by the judgment debtor to set aside the registration of a judgment under this section on such terms as the Court thinks fit; and

(c) for suspending the execution of a judgment registered under this section until the expiration of the period during which the judgment debtor may apply to have the registration set aside.

Note. In relation to Northern Ireland, for 'Rules of Court shall provide', read: 'Rules made under section seven of the Northern Ireland Act 1962, shall provide': Northern Ireland Act 1962, s 7, Sch 1.

(5) In any action brought in any Court in the United Kingdom on any judgment which might be ordered to be registered under this section, the plaintiff shall not be

---

† The operation of this part of the Act is confined to England, Scotland, and Northern Ireland, and similar provision has not yet been made as regards the Republic of Ireland.

entitled to recover any costs of the action unless an application to register the judgment under this section has previously been refused, or unless the Court otherwise orders.

10. Issue of certificates of judgments obtained in the United Kingdom. *Where a judgment has been obtained in the High Court in England or Ireland,* or in the Court of Session in Scotland, against any person, the Court shall, on an application made by the judgment creditor and on proof that the judgment debtor is resident in some part of His Majesty's dominions outside the United Kingdom to which this Part of this Act extends, issue to the judgment creditor a certified copy of the judgment.*

* This Part of the Act does *not* extend to the Republic of Ireland.

[**10.**—(1) Where—
- (a) a judgment has been obtained in the High Court in England or Northern Ireland, or in the Court of Session in Scotland, against any person; and
- (b) the judgment creditor wishes to secure the enforcement of the judgment in a part of Her Majesty's dominions outside the United Kingdom to which this Part of this Act extends,

the court shall, on an application made by the judgment creditor, issue to him a certified copy of the judgment.

(2) The reference in the preceding subsection to Her Majesty's dominions shall be construed as if that subsection had come into force in its present form at the commencement of this Act.]

Note. Section 10 in square brackets substituted for s 10 in italics by Civil Jurisdiction and Judgments Act 1982, s 35(2), as from 1 January 1987.

11. Power to make rules. Provision may be made by rules of Court for regulating the practice and procedure (including scales of fees and evidence), in respect of proceedings of any kind under this Part of this Act.†

Note. In relation to Northern Ireland, for 'Provision may be made by rules of Court', read: 'Rules may be made under section seven of the Northern Ireland Act 1962, providing': Northern Ireland Act 1962, s 7, Sch 1.

† See RSC Ord 71 (p 3956).

12. Interpretation—(1) In this Part of this Act, unless the context otherwise requires—

The expression 'judgment' means any judgment or order given or made by a Court in any civil proceedings, whether before or after the passing of this Act, whereby any sum of money is made payable, and includes an award in proceedings on an arbitration if the award has, in pursuance of the law in force in the place where it was made, become enforceable in the same manner as a judgment given by a Court in that place:

The expression 'original Court' in relation to any judgment means the Court by which the judgment was given:

The expression 'registering Court' in relation to any judgment means the Court by which the judgment was registered:

The expression 'judgment creditor' means the person by whom the judgment was obtained, and includes the successors and assigns of that person:

The expression 'judgment debtor' means the person against whom the judgment was given, and includes any person against whom the judgment is enforceable in the place where it was given.

(2) Subject to rules of Court, any of the powers conferred by this Part of this Act on any Court may be exercised by a Judge of the Court.

Note. In relation to Northern Ireland, for 'rules of Court', read: 'rules made under section seven of the Northern Ireland Act 1962': Northern Ireland Act 1962, s 7, Sch 1.

13. Power to apply Part II of Act to territories under His Majesty's Protection. His Majesty may by Order in Council declare that this Part of this Act shall apply to any territory which is under His Majesty's protection, or in respect of which a mandate is being exercised by the Government of any part of His Majesty's dominions, as if that territory were part of His Majesty's dominions, and on the making of any such Order this Part of this Act shall, subject to the provisions of the Order, have effect accordingly.*

* See note on p 2045, for places to which the Act extends.

14. Extent of Part II of Act—(1) Where His Majesty is satisfied that reciprocal provisions have been made by the legislature of any part of His Majesty's dominions outside the United Kingdom for the enforcement within that part of His dominions of judgments obtained in the High Court in England, the Court of Session in Scotland, and the High Court in Ireland, His Majesty may by Order in Council declare that this Part of this Act shall extend to that part of His dominions, and on any such Order being made this Part of this Act shall extend accordingly.†

(2) An Order in Council under this section may be varied or revoked by a subsequent Order.

[(3) Her Majesty may by Order in Council under this section consolidate any Orders in Council under this section which are in force when the consolidating Order is made.]

Note. Sub-s (3) inserted by Civil Jurisdiction and Judgments Act 1982, s 35(3), as from 24 August 1982.

† See RSC Ord 71 (p 3956).

*   *   *   *   *

MATRIMONIAL CAUSES ACT 1923*

(13 & 14 Geo 5 c 19)

An Act to amend the Matrimonial Causes Act 1857.   [*18 July 1923*]

* This Act was repealed by Supreme Court of Judicature (Consolidation) Act 1925, Sch 6.

1. Right of wife to divorce husband for adultery. *It shall be lawful for any wife to present a petition to the Court praying that her marriage may be dissolved on the ground that her husband has, since the celebration thereof and since the passing of this Act, been guilty of adultery: Provided that nothing contained herein shall affect or take away any right of any wife existing immediately before the passing of this Act.*

Note. See now Matrimonial Causes Act 1973, s 1 (p 2471), replacing Divorce Reform Act 1969, ss 1, 2 (p 2319), replacing Matrimonial Causes Act 1965, s 1(1) (p 2233), replacing Matrimonial Causes Act 1950, s 1(1) (p 2120), replacing Supreme Court of Judicature (Consolidation) Act 1925, s 176 (p 2054), as substituted by Matrimonial Causes Act 1937, s 2.

2. Amendment of 20 & 21 Vict c 85, s 27. *The provisions of the Matrimonial Causes Act 1857, set out in the Schedule to this Act are hereby repealed.*

3. Short title. *This Act may be cited as the Matrimonial Causes Act 1923, and shall be construed as one with, and may be cited with, the Matrimonial Causes Acts 1857 to 1919.*

Note. The reference to the Act of 1919 is to the temporary Matrimonial Causes (Dominions Troops) Act 1919, repealed by Statute Law Revision Act 1927.

SCHEDULE
Section twenty-seven the words 'incestuous adultery or of bigamy with', and the words 'or of adultery coupled with such cruelty as, without adultery, would have entitled her to a divorce

à mensâ et thoro, or of adultery coupled with desertion, without reasonable excuse, for two years or upwards'; and all the words in the proviso.

Note. For Matrimonial Causes Act 1857, s 27, see p 2006.

TRUSTEE ACT 1925

(15 & 16 Geo 5 c 19)

An Act to consolidate certain enactments relating to trustees in England and Wales.

[9 April 1925]

*   *   *   *   *

PART II

GENERAL POWERS OF TRUSTEES AND PERSONAL REPRESENTATIVES

*   *   *   *   *

Maintenance, Advancement and Protective Trusts

31. Power to apply income for maintenance and to accumulate surplus income during a minority—(1) Where any property is held by trustees in trust for any person for any interest whatsoever, whether vested or contingent, then, subject to any prior interests or charges affecting that property—

   (i) during the infancy of any such person, if his interest so long continues, the trustees may, at their sole discretion, pay to his parent or guardian, if any, or otherwise apply for or towards his maintenance, education, or benefit, the whole or such part, if any, of the income of that property as may, in all the circumstances, be reasonable, whether or not there is—

     (a) any other fund applicable to the same purpose; or

     (b) any person bound by law to provide for his maintenance or education; and

  (ii) if such person on attaining the age of *twenty-one years* [eighteen years] has not a vested interest in such income, the trustees shall thenceforth pay the income of that property and of any accretion thereto under subsection (2) of this section to him, until he either attains a vested interest therein or dies, or until failure of his interest:

Provided that, in deciding whether the whole or any part of the income of the property is during a minority to be paid or applied for the purposes aforesaid, the trustees shall have regard to the age of the infant and his requirements and generally to the circumstances of the case, and in particular to what other income, if any, is applicable for the same purposes; and where trustees have notice that the income of more than one fund is applicable for those purposes, then, so far as practicable, unless the entire income of the funds is paid or applied as aforesaid or the court otherwise directs, a proportionate part only of the income of each fund shall be so paid or applied.

(2) During the infancy of any such person, if his interest so long continues, the trustees shall accumulate all the residue of that income in the way of compound interest by investing the same and the resulting income thereof from time to time in authorised investments, and shall hold those accumulations as follows—

   (i) If any such person—

     (a) attains the age of *twenty-one years* [eighteen years], or marries under that age, and his interest in such income during his infancy or until his marriage is a vested interest; or

     (b) on attaining the age of *twenty-one years* [eighteen years] or on marriage under that age becomes entitled to the property from which such income arose in fee simple, absolute or determinable, or absolutely, or for an entailed interest;

the trustees shall hold the accumulations in trust for such person absolutely, but without prejudice to any provision with respect thereto contained in any settlement by him made under any statutory powers during his infancy, and so that the receipt of such person after marriage, and though still an infant, shall be a good discharge; and

(ii) In any other case the trustees shall, notwithstanding that such person had a vested interest in such income, hold the accumulations as an accretion to the capital of the property from which such accumulations arose, and as one fund with such capital for all purposes, and so that, if such property is settled land, such accumulations shall be held upon the same trusts as if the same were capital money arising therefrom;

but the trustees may, at any time during the infancy of such person if his interest so long coninues, apply those accumulations, or any part thereof, as if they were income arising in the then current year.

(3) This section applies in the case of a contingent interest only if the limitation or trust carries the intermediate income of the property, but it applies to a future or contingent legacy by the parent of, or a person standing in loco parentis to, the legatee, if and for such period as, under the general law, the legacy carries interest for the maintenance of the legatee, and in any such case as last aforesaid the rate of interest shall (if the income available is sufficient, and subject to any rules of court to the contrary) be five pounds per centum per annum.

(4) This section applies to a vested annuity in like manner as if the annuity were the income of property held by trustees in trust to pay the income thereof to the annuitant for the same period for which the annuity is payable, save that in any case accumulations made during the infancy of the annuitant shall be held in trust for the annuitant or his personal representative absolutely.

(5) This section does not apply where the instrument, if any, under which the interest arises came into operation before the commencement of this Act.

Note. The words in square brackets in sub-ss (1)(ii), (2)(i)(a), (b) were substituted by Family Law Reform Act 1969, s 1(3), Sch 1, Part I, for the words 'twenty-one years' in italics but by virtue of s 1(4) of that Act and Sch 3, para 5(1) thereto (p 2303), the amendment does not affect this section in its application to interests under instruments made before 1970 or, in its application by virtue of Administration of Estates Act 1925, s 47(1)(ii), to the estate of an intestate dying before 1970, and, by virtue of s 1(4) of the 1969 Act and Sch 3, para 9 (p 2304), the amendment does not affect the construction of any statutory provision where it is incorporated in and has effect as part of any deed, will or other instrument not otherwise affected by s 1 of that Act.

32. Power of advancement—(1) Trustees may at any time or times pay or apply any capital money subject to a trust, for the advancement or benefit, in such manner as they may, in their absolute discretion, think fit, of any person entitled to the capital of the trust property or of any share thereof, whether absolutely or contingently on his attaining any specified age or on the occurrence of any other event, or subject to a gift over on his death under any specified age or on the occurrence of any other event, and whether in possession or in remainder or reversion, and such payment or application may be made notwithstanding that the interest of such person is liable to be defeated by the exercise of a power of appointment or revocation, or to be diminished by the increase of the class to which he belongs:

Provided that—

(a) the money so paid or applied for the advancement or benefit of any person shall not exceed altogether in amount one-half of the presumptive or vested share or interest of that person in the trust property; and

(b) if that person is or becomes absolutely and indefeasibly entitled to a share in the trust property the money so paid or applied shall be brought into account as part of such share; and

(c) no such payment or application shall be made so as to prejudice any person entitled to any prior life or other interest, whether vested or contingent, in the money paid or applied unless such person is in existence and of full age and consents in writing to such payment or application.

(2) *This section applies only where the trust property consists of money or securities or of property held upon trust for sale calling in and conversion, and such money or securities, or the proceeds of such sale calling in and conversion are not by statute or in equity considered as land, or applicable as capital money for the purposes of the Settled Land Act 1925.*

[(2) This section does not apply to capital money arising under the Settled Land Act 1925.]

Note. Sub-s (2) in square brackets substituted for sub-s (2) in italics by Trusts of Land and Appointment of Trustees Act 1996, s 25(1), Sch 3, para 3(8), as from 1 January 1997.

(3) This section does not apply to trusts constituted or created before the commencement of this Act.

* * * * *

PART V

GENERAL PROVISIONS

* * * * *

68. Definitions—[(1)] In this Act, unless the context otherwise requires, the following expressions have the meanings hereby assigned to them respectively, that is to say—

(1) 'Authorised investments' mean investments authorised by the instrument, if any, creating the trust for the investment of money subject to the trust, or by law:

(2) 'Contingent right' as applied to land includes a contingent or executory interest, a possibility coupled with an interest, whether the object of the gift or limitation of the interest, or possibility is or is not ascertained, also a right of entry, whether immediate or future, and whether vested or contingent:

* * * * *

(6) 'Land' includes land of any tenure, and mines and minerals, whether or not severed from the surface, buildings or parts of buildings, whether the division is horizontal, vertical or made in any other way, and other corporeal hereditaments; also a manor, an advowson, and a rent and other incorporeal hereditaments, and an easement, right, privilege, or benefit in, over, or derived from land, *but not an undivided share in land*; and in this definition 'mines and minerals' include any strata or seam of minerals or substances in or under any land, and powers of working and getting the same, *but not an undivided share thereof*; and 'hereditaments' mean real property which under an intestacy occurring before the commencement of this Act might have devolved on an heir;

Note. Words in italics repealed by Trusts of Land and Appointment of Trustees Act 1996, s 25(2), Sch 4, as from 1 January 1997.

* * * * *

(9) 'Personal representative' means the executor, original or by representation, or administrator for the time being of a deceased person;

(10) 'Possession' includes receipt of rents and profits or the right to receive the same, if any; 'income' includes rents and profits; and 'possessed' applies to receipt of income of and to any vested estate less than a life interest in possession or in expectancy in any land;

(11) 'Property' includes real and personal property, and any estate share and interest in any property, real or personal, and any debt, and any thing in action, and any other right or interest, whether in possession or not;

(12) 'Rights' include estates and interests;

(13) 'Securities' include stocks, funds, and shares; ... and 'securities payable to bearer' include securities transferable by delivery or by delivery and endorsement;

*   *   *   *   *

(15) 'Tenant for life,' 'statutory owner,' 'settled land,' 'settlement,' 'trust instrument,' 'trustees of the settlement' ... 'term of years absolute' and 'vesting instrument' have the same meanings as in the Settled Land Act 1925, and 'entailed interest' has the same meaning as in the Law of Property Act 1925;

*   *   *   *   *

(17) 'Trust' does not include the duties incident to an estate conveyed by way of mortgage, but with this exception the expressions 'trust' and 'trustee' extend to implied and constructive trusts, and to cases where the trustee has a beneficial interest in the trust property, and to the duties incident to the office of a personal representative, and 'trustee' where the context admits, includes a personal representative, and 'new trustee' includes an additional trustee;

*   *   *   *   *

(19) 'Trust for sale' in relation to land means an immediate *binding* trust for sale, whether or not exercisable at the request or with the consent of any person, *and with or without power at discretion to postpone the sale; 'trustees for sale' mean the persons (including a personal representative) holding land on trust for sale;*

*   *   *   *   *

Note. Only the definitions of expressions used in ss 31, 32 of this Act are reproduced above. Words omitted from para (13) repealed by Administration of Justice Act 1965, s 17(1), Sch 1. Words omitted from para (15) repealed by Mental Health Act 1959, s 142(2), Sch 8, Part I. Words in italics in para (19) repealed by Trusts of Land and Appointment of Trustees Act 1996, s 25(2), Sch 4, as from 1 January 1997.

*   *   *   *   *

71. Short title, commencement, extent—(1) This Act may be cited as the Trustee Act 1925.

(2) ...

(3) This Act, except where otherwise expressly provided, extends to England and Wales only.

(4) The provisions of this Act bind the Crown.

Note. Sub-s (2) repealed by SLR Act 1950.

*   *   *   *   *

LAW OF PROPERTY ACT 1925

(15 & 16 Geo 5 c 20)

*   *   *   *   *

30. Powers of court where trustees for sale refuse to exercise powers—[*(1)*] *If the trustees for sale refuse to sell or to exercise any of the powers conferred by either of the last two sections, or any requisite consent cannot be obtained, any person interested may apply to the court for a vesting or other order for giving effect to the proposed transaction or for an order directing the trustees for sale to give effect thereto, and the court may make such order as it thinks fit.*

[*(2) The county court has jurisdiction under this section where the land which is to be dealt with in the the court does not exceed the county court limit in capital value or net annual value for rating.*]

Note. This section, as originally enacted, numbered sub-s (1), and sub-s (2) added, by County Courts Act 1984, s 148(1), Sch 2, Part II, para 2, as from 1 August 1984. Words from 'where the land' to the end in sub-s (2) repealed by High Court and County Courts Jurisdiction Order 1991, SI 1991 No 724, art 2(1), Schedule, Part I, as from 1 July 1991. This section repealed by Trusts of Land and Appointment of Trustees Act 1996, s 25(2), Sch 4, as from 1 January 1997.

*   *   *   *   *

172. Voluntary conveyances to defraud creditors voidable—(*1*) *Save as provided in this section, every conveyance of property, made whether before or after the commencement of this Act, with intent to defraud creditors, shall be voidable, at the instance of any person thereby prejudiced.*

(*2*) *This section does not affect the operation of a disentailing assurance, or the law of bankruptcy for the time being in force.*

(*3*) *This section does not extend to any estate or interest in property conveyed for valuable consideration and in good faith or upon good consideration and in good faith to any person not having, at the time of the conveyance, notice of the intent to defraud creditors.*

Note. Repealed by Insolvency Act 1985, s 235(3), Sch 10.

*   *   *   *   *

198. Registration under the Land Charges Act 1925 to be notice—(1) The registration of any instrument or matter *under the provisions of the Land Charges Act 1925 or any enactment which it replaces, in any register kept at the land registry or elsewhere* [in any register kept under the Land Charges Act 1972 or any local land charges register], shall be deemed to constitute actual notice of such instrument or matter, and of the fact of such registration, to all persons and for all purposes connected with the land affected, as from the date of registration or other prescribed date and so long as the registration continues in force.

(2) This section operates without prejudice to the provisions of this Act respecting the making of further advances by a mortgagee, and applies only to instruments and matters required or authorised to be registered *under the Land Charges Act 1925* [in any such register].

Note. Words in square brackets substituted for words in italics by Local Land Charges Act 1975, s 17(2), Sch 1, as from 1 August 1977. The reference to the 1925 Act in the heading to the section is now inapposite.

199. Restrictions on constructive notice—(1) A purchaser shall not be prejudicially affected by notice of—

(i) any instrument or matter capable of registration under the provisions of the Land Charges Act 1925, or any enactment which it replaces, which is void or not enforceable as against him under that Act or enactment, by reason of the non-registration thereof;

(ii) any other instrument or matter or any fact or thing unless-

(a) it is within his own knowledge, or would have come to his knowledge if such inquiries and inspections had been made as ought reasonably to have been made by him; or

(b) in the same transaction with respect to which a question of notice to the purchaser arises, it has come to the knowledge of his counsel, as such, or of his solicitor or other agent, as such, or would have come to the knowledge of his solicitor or other agent, as such, if such inquiries and inspections had been made as ought reasonably to have been made by the solicitor or other agent.

(2) Paragraph (ii) of the last subsection shall not exempt a purchaser from any liability under, or any obligation to perform or observe, any covenant, condition, provision, or restriction contained in any instrument under which his title is derived, mediately or immediately; and such liability or obligation may be enforced in the same manner and to the same extent as if that paragraph had not been enacted.

(3) A purchaser shall not by reason of anything in this section be affected by notice in any case where he would not have been so affected if this section had not been enacted.

(4) This section applies to purchases made either before or after the commencement of this Act.

*   *   *   *   *

SUPREME COURT OF JUDICATURE (CONSOLIDATION) ACT 1925*

(15 & 16 Geo 5 c 49)

An Act to consolidate the Judicature Acts 1873 to 1910, and other enactments relating to the Supreme Court of Judicature in England and the administration of justice therein.

[*31 July 1925*]

* Whole Act, sections of which had already been repealed and some replaced, was repealed by Supreme Court Act 1981, s 152(4), Sch 7. Only those sections of the Act which related to divorce law and practice are printed here.

32. Rules as to exercise of jurisdiction. *The jurisdiction vested in the High Court and the Court of Appeal respectively shall, so far as regards procedure and practice, be exercised in the manner provided by this Act or by rules of court, and where no special provision is contained in this Act or in rules of court with reference thereto, any such jurisdiction shall be exercised as nearly as may be in the same manner as that in which it might have been exercised by the court to which it formerly appertained.*

Note. Supreme Court of Judicature Act 1873, s 23 (p 2027), and see Matrimonial Causes Act 1857, s 22 (p 2005).

This section was restricted by Divorce Reform Act 1969, s 9(3) (p 2323) (subsequently repealed), and then repealed by Supreme Court Act 1981, s 152(4), Sch 7.

*   *   *   *   *

43. Determination of matter completely and finally. *The High Court and the Court of Appeal respectively, in the exercise of the jurisdiction vested in them by this Act, shall, in every cause or matter pending before the court, grant, either absolutely or on such terms and conditions as the court thinks just, all such remedies whatsoever as any of the parties thereto may appear to be entitled to in respect of any legal or equitable claim property brought forward by them in the cause or matter, so that, as far as possible, all matters in controversy between the parties may be completely and finally determined, and all multiplicity of legal proceedings concerning any of those matters avoided.*

Note. Supreme Court of Judicature Act 1873, s 24(7). See now Supreme Court Act 1981, s 49 (p 2789).

*   *   *   *   *

PART VIII

MATRIMONIAL CAUSES AND MATTERS

Divorce and Nullity of Marriage

176. Grounds for petition for divorce. *A petition for divorce may be presented to the High Court (in this Part of this Act referred to as 'the court')—*
- (*a*) *by a husband on the ground that his wife has since the celebration of the marriage been guilty of adultery; and*
- (*b*) *by a wife on the ground that her husband has since the celebration of the marriage been guilty of rape, or of sodomy or bestiality, or that he has since the celebration of the marriage and since the seventeenth day of July, nineteen hundred and twenty-three, been guilty of adultery:*

 Provided that nothing in this Act shall affect the right of a wife to present a petition for divorce on any ground on which she might, if the Matrimonial Causes Act 1923, had not passed, have presented such a petition, and on any petition presented by a wife for divorce on the ground of the adultery and cruelty, or adultery and desertion, of her husband, the husband and wife shall be competent and compellable to give evidence with respect to the cruelty or desertion.

Note. A new s 176 was substituted for the section printed above by Matrimonial Causes Act 1937, s 2. The substituted section was repealed by Matrimonial Causes Act 1950, s 34(1), Schedule. See now Matrimonial Causes Act 1973, s 1(1), (2) (p 2471), replacing Divorce Reform Act 1969, ss 1, 2(1) (p 2319), replacing Matrimonial Causes Act 1965, s 1(1) (p 2223), replacing Matrimonial Causes Act 1950, s 1(1) (p 2120).

 For former law, see Matrimonial Causes Act 1857, s 27 (p 2006); Matrimonial Causes Act 1859, s 6 (p 2019); Matrimonial Causes Act 1923 (p 2048).

177. Provision as to making adulterer co-respondent—(*1*) *On a petition for divorce presented by the husband or in the answer of a husband praying for divorce the petitioner or respondent, as the case may be, shall make the alleged adulterer a co-respondent unless he is excused by the court on special grounds from so doing.*

 (*2*) *On a petition for divorce presented by the wife the court may, if it thinks fit, direct that the person with whom the husband is alleged to have committed adultery be made a respondent.*

Note. Repealed by Matrimonial Causes Act 1950, s 34(1), Schedule. See now Matrimonial Causes Act 1973, s 49 (p 2522), replacing Matrimonial Causes Act 1965, s 4 (p 2225), replacing Matrimonial Causes Act 1950, s 3 (p 2122).

178. Duty of court on presentation of petition—[(*1*) *On a petition for divorce it shall be the duty of the court to satisfy itself so far as it reasonably can both as to the facts alleged and also as to whether the petitioner has been accessory to or has connived at or condoned the adultery or not, and also to enquire into any countercharge which is made against the petitioner.*

 (*2*) *If on the evidence the court is not satisfied that the alleged adultery has been committed or finds that the petitioner has during the marriage been accessory to or has connived at or condoned the adultery complained of, or that the petition is presented or prosecuted in collusion with either of the respondents, the court shall dismiss the petition.*

 (*3*) *If the court is satisfied on the evidence that the case for the petition has been proved and does not find that the petitioner has in any manner been accessory to or connived at or condoned the adultery or that the petition is presented or prosecuted in collusion with either of the respondents, the court shall pronounce a decree of divorce:*

 Provided that the court shall not be bound to pronounce a decree of divorce if it finds that the petitioner has during the marriage been guilty of adultery, or if in the opinion of the court he has been guilty—

 (*a*) *of unreasonable delay in presenting or prosecuting the petition; or*

 (*b*) *of cruelty towards the other party to the marriage; or*

 (*c*) *of having without reasonable excuse deserted, or of having without reasonable excuse wilfully separated himself or herself from, the other party before the adultery complained of; or*

 (*d*) *of such wilful neglect or misconduct as has conduced to the adultery*].

178.—(*1*) *On a petition for divorce it shall be the duty of the court to inquire, so far as it reasonably can into the facts alleged and whether there has been any connivance or condonation on the part of the petitioner and whether any collusion exists between the parties and also to inquire into any countercharge which is made against the petitioner.*

 (*2*) *If the court is satisfied on the evidence that—*

  (*i*) *the case for the petition has been proved; and*

  (*ii*) *where the ground of the petition is adultery, the petitioner has not in any manner been accessory to, or connived at, or condoned the adultery, or where the ground of the petition is cruelty the petitioner has not in any manner condoned the cruelty; and*

  (*iii*) *the petition is not presented or prosecuted in collusion with the respondent or either of the respondents,* the court shall pronounce a decree of divorce, but if the court is not satisfied with respect to any of the aforesaid matters, it shall dismiss the petition:

Provided that the court shall not be bound to pronounce a decree of divorce and may dismiss the petition if it finds that the petitioner has during the marriage been guilty of adultery or if, in the opinion of the court, the petitioner has been guilty—

(a) of unreasonable delay in presenting or prosecuting the petition; or

(b) of cruelty towards the other party to the marriage; or

(c) where the ground of the petition is adultery or cruelty, of having without reasonable excuse deserted, or having without reasonable excuse wilfully separated himself or herself from, the other party before the adultery or cruelty complained of; or

(d) where the ground of the petition is adultery or unsoundness of mind or desertion, of such wilful neglect or misconduct as has conduced to the adultery or unsoundness of mind or desertion.

Note. Section 178 in square brackets substituted for section printed above by Matrimonial Causes Act 1937, s 4. The substituted section was repealed by Matrimonial Causes Act 1950, s 34(1), Schedule. See now Matrimonial Causes Act 1973, ss 1(3), (4), 2(1), (3) (p 2471), replacing Divorce Reform Act 1969, ss 2(2), (3), 3(3), (4) (pp 2319, 2320), replacing Matrimonial Causes Act 1965, s 5 (p 2225), replacing Matrimonial Causes Act 1950, s 4 (p 2122), as amended by Matrimonial Causes Act 1963, s 4.

For former statutory provisions, see Matrimonial Causes Act 1857, ss 29, 30, 31 (p 2007).

179. Dismissal of respondent or co-respondent from proceedings. *In any case in which, on the petition of a husband for divorce, the alleged adulterer is made a co-respondent or in which, on the petition of a wife for divorce, the person with whom the husband is alleged to have committed adultery is made a respondent, the court may, after the close of the evidence on the part of the petitioner, direct the co-respondent or the respondent, as the case may be, to be dismissed from the proceedings if the court is of opinion that there is not sufficient evidence against him or her.*

Note. Repealed by Matrimonial Causes Act 1950, s 34(1), Schedule. See now Matrimonial Causes Act 1973, s 49(3) (p 2522), replacing Matrimonial Causes Act 1965, s 4(3) (p 2225), replacing Matrimonial Causes Act 1950, s 5 (p 2122).

For former statutory provision, see Matrimonial Causes Act 1858, s 11 (p 2016).

180. Relief to respondent on petition for divorce. *If in any proceedings for divorce the respondent opposes the relief sought, in the case of proceedings instituted by the husband, on the ground of his adultery, cruelty or desertion, or, in the case of proceedings instituted by the wife, on the ground of her adultery, cruelty or desertion, the court may give to the respondent the same relief to which he or she would have been entitled if he or she had presented a petition seeking such relief.*

Note. Repealed by Matrimonial Causes Act 1950, s 34(1), Schedule. See now Matrimonial Causes Act 1973, s 20 (p 2481), replacing Matrimonial Causes Act 1965, s 5(6) (p 2225), replacing Matrimonial Causes Act 1950, s 6 (p 2122).

For former statutory provision, see Matrimonial Causes Act 1866, s 2 (p 2022).

181. Duties of King's Proctor. *In the case of any petition for divorce or for nullity of marriage—*

(1) *The court may, if it thinks fit, direct all necessary papers in the matter to be sent to His Majesty's Proctor, who shall under the directions of the Attorney-General instruct counsel to argue before the court any question in relation to the matter which the court deems to be necessary or expedient to have fully argued, and His Majesty's Proctor shall be entitled to charge the costs of the proceedings as part of the expenses of his office:*

(2) *Any person may at any time during the progress of the proceedings or before the decree nisi is made absolute give information to His Majesty's Proctor of any matter material to the due decision of the case, and His Majesty's Proctor may thereupon take such steps as the Attorney-General considers necessary or expedient:*

(3) *If in consequence of any such information or otherwise His Majesty's Proctor suspects that any parties to the petition are or have been acting in collusion for the purpose of obtaining a decree contrary to the justice of the case, he may, under the direction of the Attorney-General, after obtaining the leave of the court, intervene and retain counsel and subpœna witnesses to prove the alleged collusion.*

Note. Repealed by Matrimonial Causes Act 1950, s 34(1), Schedule. See now Matrimonial Causes Act 1973, ss 8(1), 15 (pp 2475, 2478), replacing Matrimonial Causes Act 1965, ss 6(1), 10 (pp 2227, 2229), replacing Matrimonial Causes Act 1950, s 10 (p 2124).

For former statutory provisions, see Matrimonial Causes Act 1860, ss 5, 7 (p 2020); Matrimonial Causes Act 1873, s 1 (p 2027).

182. Provisions as to costs where King's Proctor intervenes or shows cause—
(*1*) *Where His Majesty's Proctor intervenes or shows cause against a decree nisi in any proceedings for divorce or for nullity of marriage, the court may make such order as to the payment by other parties to the proceedings of the costs incurred by him in so doing or as to the payment by him of any costs incurred by any of the said parties by reason of his so doing, as may seem just.*

(*2*) *So far as the reasonable costs incurred by His Majesty's Proctor in so intervening or showing cause are not fully satisfied by any order made under this section for the payment of his costs, he shall be entitled to charge the difference as part of the expenses of his office, and the Treasury may, if they think fit, order that any costs which under any order made by the court under this section His Majesty's Proctor pays to any parties shall be deemed to be part of the expenses of his office.*

Note. Repealed by Matrimonial Causes Act 1950, s 34(1), Schedule. See now Matrimonial Causes Act 1973, ss 8(2), (3), 15 (pp 2475, 2478), replacing Matrimonial Causes Act 1965, ss 6(2), (3), 10 (pp 2227, 2229), replacing Matrimonial Causes Act 1950, s 11 (p 2124).

For former statutory provisions, see Matrimonial Causes Act 1860, s 7 (p 2020); Matrimonial Causes Act 1878, s 2 (p 2028).

183. Decree nisi for divorce or nullity of marriage—(*1*) *Every decree for a divorce or for nullity of marriage shall, in the first instance, be a decree nisi not to be made absolute until after the expiration of six months from the pronouncing thereof, unless the court by general or special order from time to time fixes a shorter time.*

(*2*) *After the pronouncing of the decree nisi and before the decree is made absolute, any person may, in the prescribed manner, show cause why the decree should not be made absolute by reason of the decree having been obtained by collusion or by reason of material facts not having been brought before the court, and in any such case the court may make the decree absolute, reverse the decree nisi, require further inquiry or otherwise deal with the case as the court thinks fit.*

[(*3*) *Where a decree nisi has been obtained, whether before or after the passing of this Act, and no application for the decree to be made absolute has been made by the party who obtained the decree, then at any time after the expiration of three months from the earliest date on which that party could have made such an application, the party against whom the decree nisi has been granted shall be at liberty to apply to the court and the court shall, on such application, have power to make the decree absolute, reverse the decree nisi, require further inquiry or otherwise deal with the case as the court thinks fit.*]

Note. Sub-s (3) added by Matrimonial Causes Act 1937, s 9. The whole section, as amended, repealed by Matrimonial Causes Act 1950, s 34(1), Schedule. See now Matrimonial Causes Act 1973, ss 1(5), 9, 15 (pp 2471, 2475, 2478), replacing Matrimonial Causes Act 1965, ss 5(7), 7, 10 (pp 2225, 2227, 2229), replacing Matrimonial Causes Act 1950, s 12 (p 2124).

For former statutory provisions, see Matrimonial Causes Act 1860, s 7 (p 2020); Matrimonial Causes Act 1866, s 3 (p 2022); Matrimonial Causes Act 1873, s 1 (p 2027).

184. Re-marriage of divorced persons—(*1*) *As soon as any decree for divorce is made absolute, either of the parties to the marriage may, if there is no right of appeal against the decree absolute, marry again as if the prior marriage had been dissolved by death or, if there is such a right of appeal, may so marry again, if no appeal is presented against the decree, as soon as the time for appealing has expired, or, if an appeal is so presented, as soon as the appeal has been dismissed:*

Provided that it shall be lawful for a man to marry the sister or half-sister of his divorced wife or of his wife by whom he has been divorced during the lifetime of the wife, or the divorced wife of his brother or half-brother or the wife of his brother or half-brother who has divorced his brother during the lifetime of the brother or half-brother.

Note. The following proviso was substituted for the one printed above by Marriage (Prohibited Degrees of Relationship) Act 1931, s 2:

[*Provided that it shall not be unlawful for a man to contract any marriage which, upon the decease of any person, would be authorised by the Marriage (Prohibited Degrees of Relationship) Acts 1907 to 1931 (as amended by any subsequent enactment) but which would otherwise have been void or voidable by reason of affinity, during the lifetime of that person.*]

(*2*) *No clergyman of the Church of England shall be compelled to solemnise the marriage of any person whose former marriage has been dissolved on the ground of his or her adultery, or shall be liable to any proceedings, penalty or censure for solemnising or refusing to solemnise the marriage of any such person.*

(*3*) *If any minister of any church or chapel of the Church of England refuses to perform the marriage service between any persons who but for his refusal would be entitled to have the service performed in that church or chapel, he shall permit any other minister of the Church of England entitled to officiate within the diocese in which the church or chapel is situate to perform the marriage service in that church or chapel.*

[(*2*) *No clergyman of the Church of England or of the Church in Wales shall be compelled to solemnize the marriage of any person whose former marriage has been dissolved on any ground and whose former husband or wife is still living or to permit the marriage of any such person in the Church or Chapel of which he is the minister.*]

Note. Sub-ss (2), (3) repealed and replaced by new sub-s (2) in square brackets by Matrimonial Causes Act 1937, s 12. The section, as amended, repealed by Matrimonial Causes Act 1950, s 34(1), Schedule, and replaced by s 13 of that Act (p 2125). See Matrimonial Causes Act 1965, s 8 (p 2228).

For former statutory provisions, see Matrimonial Causes Act 1857, ss 57, 58 (p 2012); Matrimonial Causes Act 1868, s 4 (p 2023); Deceased Wife's Sister's Marriage Act 1907, ss 3(2), 5; Deceased Brother's Widow's Marriage Act 1921, s 1(2)(b), (4). See also Marriage Act 1949 (p 2100); and Marriage (Enabling) Act 1960.

Judicial Separation and Restitution of Conjugal Rights

185. Decree for judicial separation—(*1*) *A petition for judicial separation may be presented to the court either by the husband or the wife on the ground of adultery or cruelty, desertion without cause for not less than two years, failure to comply with a decree for restitution of conjugal rights, or on any ground on which a decree for divorce a mensa et thoro might have been pronounced immediately before the commencement of the Matrimonial Causes Act 1857.*

(*2*) *The court may, on being satisfied that the allegations contained in the petition are true and that there is no legal ground why the petition should not be granted, make a decree for judicial separation, and any such decree shall have the same force and effect as a decree for divorce a mensa et thoro had immediately before the commencement of the Matrimonial Causes Act 1857.*

[(*1*) *A petition for judicial separation may be presented to the court either by the husband or the wife on any grounds on which a petition for divorce might have been presented, or on the ground of failure to comply with a decree for restitution of conjugal rights or on any ground on which a decree for divorce a mensa et thoro might have been pronounced immediately before the commencement of the Matrimonial Causes Act 1857, and the foregoing provisions of this Part of the Act relating to the duty of the court on the presentation of a petition for divorce, and the circumstances in which such a petition shall or may be granted or dismissed, shall apply in like manner to a petition for judicial separation.*

(*2*) *Where the court in accordance with the said provisions grants a decree of judicial separation, it shall no longer be obligatory for the petitioner to cohabit with the respondent.*]

Note. Sub-ss (1), (2) replaced by new sub-ss (1), (2) in square brackets by Matrimonial Causes Act 1937, s 5.

(*3*) *The court may, on the application by petition of the husband or wife against whom a decree for judicial separation has been made, and on being satisfied that the allegations contained in the petition are true, reverse the decree at any time after the making thereof, on the ground that it was obtained in the absence of the person making the application, or, if desertion was the ground of the decree, that there was reasonable cause for the alleged desertion.*

(*4*) *The reversal of a decree for judicial separation shall not affect the rights or remedies which any other person would have had if the decree had not been reversed in respect of any debts, contracts or acts of the wife incurred, entered into or done between that date of the decree and of the reversal thereof.*

Note. As stated, sub-ss (1) and (2) repealed and replaced by Matrimonial Causes Act 1937, s 5. The substituted subsections and sub-s (3) repealed by Matrimonial Causes Act 1950, s 34(1), Schedule. See now Matrimonial Causes Act 1973, ss 17, 18 (pp 2479, 2480), replacing Matrimonial Causes Act 1965, s 12 (p 2229), replacing Matrimonial Causes Act 1950, s 14 (p 2125). Sub-s (4) repealed by the 1950 Act and not replaced.

For former statutory provisions, see Matrimonial Causes Act 1857, ss 7, 16, 17, 23 (pp 2002, 2003–2004, 2005); Matrimonial Causes Act 1884, s 5 (p 2033).

186. Decree for restitution of conjugal rights. *A petition for restitution of conjugal rights may be presented to the court either by the husband or the wife, and the court, on being satisfied that the allegations contained in the petition are true, and that there is no legal ground why a decree for restitution of conjugal rights should not be granted, may make the decree accordingly.*

Note. Repealed by Matrimonial Causes Act 1950, s 34(1), Schedule and re-enacted by ibid, s 15(1) (p 2125), which was replaced by Matrimonial Causes Act 1965, s 13(1) (p 2230), which was repealed but not replaced by Matrimonial Proceedings and Property Act 1970, s 42(2), Sch 3. See also Act of 1970, s 20 (p 2357).

For former statutory provision, see Matrimonial Causes Act 1857, s 17 (p 2004).

187. Periodical payments in lieu of attachment—(*1*) *A decree for restitution of conjugal rights shall not be enforced by attachment, but where the application is by the wife the court, at the time of making the decree or at any time afterwards, may, in the event of the decree not being complied with within any time in that behalf limited by the court, order the respondent to make to the petitioner such periodical payments as may be just, and the order may be enforced in the same manner as an order for alimony in proceedings for judicial separation.*

Note. Repealed by Matrimonial Causes Act 1950, s 34(1), Schedule, and re-enacted by ibid, ss 15(2), 22(3) (pp 2125, 2129), which were replaced by Matrimonial Causes Act 1965, ss 13(2), 21(1), (2) (pp 2230, 2233), which were repealed but not replaced by Matrimonial Proceedings and Property Act 1970, s 42(2), Sch 3.

(*2*) *The court may, if it thinks fit, order that the husband shall, to the satisfaction of the court, secure to the wife the periodical payments, and for that purpose may direct that it shall be referred to one of the conveyancing counsel of the court to settle and approve a proper deed or instrument to be executed by all necessary parties.*

Note. Repealed by Matrimonial Causes Act 1950, s 34(1), Schedule. See now Matrimonial Causes Act 1973, s 27 (p 2496), replacing Matrimonial Proceedings and Property Act 1970, s 6 (p 2348), replacing Matrimonial Causes Act 1965, s 22(2) (p 2234), replacing Matrimonial Causes Act 1950, s 22(4) (p 2130).

For former statutory provision, see Matrimonial Causes Act 1884, s 2 (p 2032). See also Administration of Justice (Miscellaneous Provisions) Act 1938, s 14.

Legitimacy Declarations

188. Declaration of legitimacy, &c. (*1*) *Any person who is a natural-born subject of His Majesty, or whose right to be deemed a natural-born subject of His Majesty depends wholly or in part on his legitimacy or on the validity of any marriage, may, if he is domiciled in England or Northern Ireland or claims any real or personal estate situate in England, apply by petition to the court for a decree declaring that the petitioner is the legitimate child of his parents, and that the marriage of his father and mother or of the grandfather and grandmother was a valid marriage or that his own marriage was a valid marriage.*

(*2*) *Any person who is so domiciled or claims as aforesaid, may apply to the court for a decree declaring his right to be deemed a natural-born subject of His Majesty.*

(*3*) *Applications under subsections (1) and (2) of this section may be included in the same petition and on any such application the court shall make such decree as the court thinks just, and the decree shall be binding on His Majesty and all other persons whatsoever:*

Provided that the decree of the court shall not prejudice any person—

(i)   *if it is subsequently proved to have been obtained by fraud or collusion; or*

(ii)   *unless that person has been cited or made a party to the proceedings or is the heir-at-law, next of kin, or other real or personal representative of, or derives title under or through, a person so cited or made a party.*

(4)   *A copy of every petition under this section and of any affidavit accompanying the petition shall be delivered to the Attorney-General at least one month before the petition is presented or filed, and the Attorney-General shall be a respondent on the hearing of the petition and on any subsequent proceedings relating thereto.*

(5)   *In any application under this section such persons shall, subject to rules of court, be cited to see proceedings or otherwise summoned as the court shall think fit, and any such persons may be permitted to become parties to the proceedings and to oppose the application.*

(6)   *The provisions of this Act relating to matrimonial causes shall, so far as applicable, extend to any proceedings under this section.*

(7)   *No proceedings under this section shall affect any final judgment or decree already pronounced or made by any court of competent jurisdiction.*

Note. Words 'natural-born' in sub-ss (1), (2) repealed by British Nationality Act 1948, Sch IV. The whole section repealed by Matrimonial Causes Act 1950, s 34(1), Schedule. See now Matrimonial Causes Act 1973, s 45 (p 2520), replacing Matrimonial Causes Act 1965, s 39 (p 2246), replacing Matrimonial Causes Act 1950, s 17, as amended (p 2126).

For former statutory provision, see Legitimacy Declaration Act 1858, ss 1, 2, 4, 6–8. See also Legitimacy Act 1926, s 2(1), and Administration of Justice (Miscellaneous Provisions) Act 1933, s 7(1).

Miscellaneous

189. Damages—(*1*) *A husband may on a petition for divorce or for judicial separation or for damages only, claim damages from any person on the ground of adultery with the wife of the petitioner.*

(2)   *A claim for damages on the ground of adultery shall, subject to the provisions of any enactment relating to trial by jury in the court, be tried on the same principles and in the same manner as actions for criminal conversation were tried immediately before the commencement of the Matrimonial Causes Act 1857, and the provisions of this Act with reference to the hearing and decision of petitions shall so far as may be necessary apply to the hearing and decision of petitions on which damages are claimed.*

(3)   *The court may direct in what manner the damages recovered on any such petition are to be paid or applied, and may direct the whole or any part of the damages to be settled for the benefit of the children, if any, of the marriage, or as a provision for the maintenance of the wife.*

Note. Repealed by Matrimonial Causes Act 1950, s 34(1), Schedule and replaced by ibid, s 30 (p 2132), subsequently replaced by Matrimonial Causes Act 1965, s 41 (p 2247) and finally repealed by Law Reform (Miscellaneous Provisions) Act 1970, ss 4, 7(2), Schedule.

For former statutory provision, see Matrimonial Causes Act 1857, s 33 (p 2008).

190. Alimony [sic]—(*1*) *The court may, if it thinks fit, on any decree for divorce or nullity of marriage, order that the husband shall, to the satisfaction of the court, secure to the wife such gross sum of money or annual sum of money for any term, not exceeding her life, as having regard to her fortune, if any, to the ability of her husband and to the conduct of the parties, the court may deem to be reasonable, and the court may for that purpose order that it shall be referred to one of the conveyancing counsel of the court to settle and approve a proper deed or instrument, to be executed by all the necessary parties, and may, if it thinks fit, suspend the pronouncing of the decree until the deed or instrument has been duly executed.*

(2)   *In any such case as aforesaid the court may, if it thinks fit by order, either in addition to or instead of an order under subsection (1) of this section, direct the husband to pay to the wife during the joint lives of the husband and wife such monthly or weekly sum for her maintenance and support as the court may think reasonable:*

Provided that—

(a) if the husband, after any such order has been made, becomes from any cause unable to make the payments, the court may discharge or modify the order, or temporarily suspend the order as to the whole or any part of the money ordered to be paid, and subsequently revive it wholly or in part as the court thinks fit; and

(b) where the court has made any such order as is mentioned in this subsection and the court is satisfied that the means of the husband have increased, the court may, if it thinks fit, increase the amount payable under the order.

Note. Words 'Provided that' to end of subsection repealed by Administration of Justice (Miscellaneous Provisions) Act 1938, s 20, Fourth Schedule.

Remainder of sub-s (2), and sub-s (1) repealed, and replaced by Matrimonial Causes Act 1950, s 34(1), Schedule. See now Matrimonial Causes Act 1973, s 23 (p 2489), replacing Matrimonial Proceedings and Property Act 1970, s 2 (p 2345), replacing Matrimonial Causes Act 1965, ss 16(1), (2), 19 (pp 2231, 2232), replacing Matrimonial Causes Act 1950, s 19(2), (3) (p 2128).

(3) *On any petition for divorce or nullity of marriage the court shall have the same power to make interim orders for the payment of money by way of alimony or otherwise to the wife as the court has in proceedings for judicial separation.*

Note. Repealed by Matrimonial Causes Act 1950, s 34(1), Schedule. See now Matrimonial Causes Act 1973, s 22 (p 2482) replacing Matrimonial Proceedings and Property Act 1970, s 1 (p 2345), replacing Matrimonial Causes Act 1965, s 15 (p 2230), replacing Matrimonial Causes Act 1950, ss 19(1), 20(1), 22(1) (pp 2128, 2129).

(4) *Where any decree for restitution of conjugal rights or judicial separation is made on the application of the wife, the court may make such order for alimony as the court thinks just.*

Note. Repealed by Matrimonial Causes Act 1950, s 34(1), Schedule and replaced by ibid, ss 20(2), 22(2) (p 2129), which were replaced by Matrimonial Causes Act 1965, s 20(1) (p 2232) (replaced by Matrimonial Proceedings and Property Act 1970, ss 2, 21(1) (pp 2345, 2357) (repealed but not replaced by ibid, ss 20, 42(2), Sch 3). See now Matrimonial Causes Act 1973, s 23 (p 2484).

(5) *In all cases where the court makes an order for alimony, the court may direct the alimony to be paid either to the wife or to a trustee approved by the court on her behalf, and may impose such terms or restrictions as the court thinks expedient, and may from time to time appoint a new trustee if for any reason it appears to the court expedient so to do.*

Note. Repealed by Matrimonial Causes Act 1950, s 34(1), Schedule and replaced by ibid, s 27(1) (p 2131), replaced by Matrimonial Causes Act 1965, s 30(1) (p 2240), which was repealed but not replaced by Matrimonial Proceedings and Property Act 1970, s 42(2), Sch 3.

For former statutory provisions, see Matrimonial Causes Act 1857, ss 17, 24 (pp 2004, 2005); Matrimonial Causes Act 1907, s 1 (p 2034). See also Matrimonial Causes Act 1937, s 10 (p 2091).

191. Power of court to order settlement of wife's property—(*1*) *If it appears to the court in any case in which the court pronounces a decree for divorce or for judicial separation by reason of the adultery,* [*desertion, or cruelty*] *of the wife that the wife is entitled to any property either in possession or reversion, the court may, if it thinks fit, order such settlement as it thinks reasonable to be made of the property, or any part thereof, for the benefit of the innocent party, and of the children of the marriage or any or either of them.*

Any instrument made under any order of the court made under this section shall be valid and effectual, notwithstanding the existence of coverture at the time of the execution thereof.

Note. Words in square brackets inserted by Matrimonial Causes Act 1937, s 10(3).

Repealed by Matrimonial Causes Act 1950, s 34(1), Schedule. See now Matrimonial Causes Act 1973, s 24 (p 2487), replacing Matrimonial Proceedings and Property Act 1970, s 4 (p 2346), replacing Matrimonial Causes Act 1965, ss 17(2), 20(2) (pp 2231, 2232), replacing Matrimonial Causes Act 1950, s 24(1) (p 2130).

For former statutory provisions, see Matrimonial Causes Act 1857, s 45 (p 2010); Matrimonial Causes Act 1860, ss 6, 7 (p 2020). See also Matrimonial Causes Act 1937, s 10 (p 2091), and Administration of Justice (Miscellaneous Provisions) Act 1938.

(*2*) *Where the application for restitution of conjugal rights is by the husband, and it appears to the court that the wife is entitled to any property, either in possession or reversion, or is in receipt of any profits of trade or earnings, the court may, if it thinks fit, order a settlement to be made to the satisfaction of the court of the property or any part thereof for the benefit of the petitioner and of the children of the marriage or either or any of them or may order such part of the profits of trade or earnings, as the court thinks reasonable, to be periodically paid by the respondent to the petitioner for his own benefit, or to the petitioner or any other person for the benefit of the children of the marriage, or either or any of them.*

Note. Repealed by Matrimonial Causes Act 1950, s 34(1), Schedule, and replaced by ibid, s 24(2) (p 2130), which was replaced by Matrimonial Causes Act 1965, s 21(3) (p 2233), which was finally repealed but not replaced by Matrimonial Proceedings and Property Act 1970, ss 20, 42(2), Sch 3.

For former statutory provision, see Matrimonial Causes Act 1884, s 3 (p 2032).

192. Power of court to make order as to application of settled property. *The court may after pronouncing a decree for divorce or for nullity of marriage inquire into the existence of ante-nuptial or post-nuptial settlements made on the parties whose marriage is the subject of the decree, and may make such orders with reference to the application of the whole or any part of the property settled either for the benefit of the children of the marriage or of the parties to the marriage, as the court thinks fit, and the court may exercise the powers conferred by this subsection notwithstanding that there are no children of the marriage.*

Note. Repealed by Matrimonial Causes Act 1950, s 34(1), Schedule. See now Matrimonial Causes Act 1973, ss 24, 52(1) (pp 2488, 2525), replacing Matrimonial Proceedings and Property Act 1970, ss 4, 27(1) (pp 2346, 2359), replacing Matrimonial Causes Act 1965, ss 17(1), 19, 46(2) (pp 2231, 2232, 2249), replacing Matrimonial Causes Act 1950, s 25 (p 2131).

For former statutory provisions, see Matrimonial Causes Act 1859, s 5 (p 2018); Matrimonial Causes Act 1878, s 3 (p 2028). See also Matrimonial Causes Act 1937, s 10 (p 2091).

193. Custody of children—(*1*) *In any proceedings for divorce or nullity of marriage or judicial separation, the court may from time to time, either before or by or after the final decree, make such provision as appears just with respect to the custody, maintenance and education of the children, the marriage of whose parents is the subject of the proceedings, or, if it thinks fit, direct proper proceedings to be taken for placing the children under the protection of the court.*

Note. Repealed by Matrimonial Causes Act 1950, s 34(1), Schedule. See now Matrimonial Causes Act 1973, ss 23, 42, 52(1) (pp 2484, 2518, 2525), replacing Matrimonial Proceedings and Property Act 1970, ss 3, 18, 27(1) (pp 2346, 2356, 2359), replacing Matrimonial Causes Act 1965, ss 34(1), (4), 46(2) (pp 2242, 2249), replacing Matrimonial Causes Act 1950, s 26(1) (p 2131).

For former statutory provisions, see Matrimonial Causes Act 1857, s 35 (p 2008); Matrimonial Causes Act 1859, s 4 (p 2018). See also Guardianship of Minors Act 1971, s 1 and Guardianship Act 1973.

(*2*) *On an application made in that behalf the court may, at any time before final decree, in any proceedings for restitution of conjugal rights, or, if the respondent fails to comply therewith, after final decree, make from time to time all such orders and provisions with respect to the custody, maintenance and education of the children of the petitioner and respondent as might have been made by interim orders if proceedings for judicial separation had been pending between the same parties.*

[(*3*) *The court may, if it thinks fit, on any decree of divorce or nullity of marriage, order the husband, or (in the case of a petition for divorce by a wife on the ground of her husband's insanity) order the wife, to secure for the benefit of the children such gross sum of money or annual sum of money as the court may deem reasonable, and the court may for that purpose order that it shall be referred to one of the conveyancing counsel of the court to settle and approve a proper deed or instrument to be executed by all necessary parties:*

Provided that the term for which any sum of money is secured for the benefit of a child shall not extend beyond the date when the child will attain twenty-one years of age.]

Note. Sub-s (3) added by Matrimonial Causes Act 1937, s 10(4). Section as amended repealed by Matrimonial Causes Act 1950, s 34(1), Schedule, re-enacted by ibid, s 26(2), (3) (p 2131), replaced by Matrimonial Causes Act 1965, ss 34(1), (3), (4), 46(2) (pp 2242, 2249). See Matrimonial Proceedings and Property Act 1970, ss 3, 18, 20 (abolition of right to claim restitution of conjugal rights), 27(1), 42(2), Sch 3 (pp 2346, 2356, 2357, 2359, 2364, 2368), replaced by Matrimonial Causes Act 1973, ss 23, 42, 52 and the notes thereto (pp 2484, 2518, 2525).

See also Matrimonial Causes Act 1973, s 10(1) (p 2476).

For former statutory provision, see Matrimonial Causes Act 1884, s 6 (p 2033). See also Guardianship of Minors Act 1971, s 1 and Guardianship Act 1973.

194. Wife's property in a case of judicial separation—(*1*) *In every case of judicial separation*—

(*a*) *the wife shall, as from the date of the decree and so long as the separation continue, be considered as a feme sole with respect to any property which she may acquire or which may devolve upon her, and any such property may be disposed of by her in all respects as a feme sole and if she dies intestate shall devolve as if her husband had been then dead; and*

(*b*) *the wife shall, during the separation, be considered as a feme sole for the purpose of contract and wrongs and injuries, and of suing and being sued, and the husband shall not be liable in respect of her contracts or for any wrongful act or omission by her or for any costs she incurs as plaintiff or defendant:*

> *Provided that—*

(*i*) *where on any judicial separation alimony has been ordered to be paid and has not been duly paid by the husband, he shall be liable for necessaries supplied for the use of the wife;*

(*ii*) *if the wife returns to cohabitation with her husband, any property to which she is entitled at the date of her return shall, subject to any agreement in writing made between herself and her husband while separate, be her separate property;*

(*iii*) *nothing in this section shall prevent the wife from joining at any time during the separation in the exercise of any joint power given to herself and her husband.*

[(*1*) *In every case of judicial separation*—

(*a*) *as from the date of the decree and so long as the separation continues any property which is acquired by or devolves upon the wife shall not be affected by any restraint upon anticipation attached to the enjoyment by the wife of any property under any settlement, agreement for a settlement, will, or other instrument; and if she dies intestate shall devolve as if her husband had been then dead;*

(*b*) *if alimony has been ordered to be paid and has not been duly paid by the husband he shall be liable for necessaries supplied for the use of the wife.*]

Note. New sub-s (1) in square brackets substituted by Law Reform (Married Women and Tortfeasors) Act 1935, s 5(1), Sch 1, and para (a) of the substituted subsection replaced by Married Women (Restraint Upon Anticipation) Act 1949, s 1(2), Sch 1 (pp 2118, 2119): 'any property which is acquired by or devolves upon the wife on or after the date of the decree whilst the separation continues shall, if she dies intestate, devolve as if her husband had then been dead'.

The amended and substituted subsection repealed by Matrimonial Causes Act 1950, s 34(1), Schedule and replaced by ibid, s 21(1) (p 2129), replaced by Matrimonial Causes Act 1965, s 20(3), (4) (p 2232), which was repealed (with saving for s 20(3)) by Matrimonial Proceedings and Property Act 1970, s 42(2), Sch 3 (pp 2364, 2368). See now Matrimonial Causes Act 1973, s 18(2) (p 2480), replacing s 40(1) of the Act of 1970 (p 2363).

(*2*) *In any case where the decree for judicial separation is obtained by the wife, any property to which she is entitled for an estate in remainder or reversion at the date of the decree, and any property to which she becomes entitled as executrix, administratrix or trustee after the date of the decree, shall be deemed to be property to which this section applies, and for the purpose aforesaid the death of the testator or intestate shall be deemed to be the date when the wife became entitled as executrix or administratrix.*

Note. Repealed and replaced by Matrimonial Causes Act 1950, s 21(2) (p 2129), replaced by Matrimonial Causes Act 1965, s 20(3) (p 2232), which was repealed (with saving) by Matrimonial Proceedings and Property Act 1970, s 42(2), Sch 3 (pp 2364, 2368).

2064   Supreme Court of Judicature (Consolidation) Act 1925, s 194

For former statutory provisions, see Matrimonial Causes Act 1857, ss 25, 26 (pp 2005, 2006); Matrimonial Causes Act 1858, ss 7, 8 (p 2015).

195. Protection of third parties—(*1*) *Where a wife obtains a decree for judicial separation, the decree shall, so far as may be necessary for the protection of any person dealing with the wife, be valid and effectual until discharged, and the discharge or variation of the decree shall not affect any rights or remedies which any person would have had, if the decree had not been discharged or varied, in respect of any debts, contracts or acts of the wife incurred, entered into or done during the period between the date of the decree and the discharge or variation thereof.*

(*2*) *Any person who, in reliance on any such decree as aforesaid, makes any payment to or permits any transfer or act to be made or done by the wife, shall, notwithstanding the subsequent discharge or variation of the decree, or the fact that the separation has ceased or has been discontinued, be protected and indemnified in the same way in all respects as if at the time of the payment, transfer or other act the decree were valid and still subsisting without variation in full force and effect, or the separation had not ceased or been discontinued, as the case may be, unless at that time that person had notice of the discharge or variation of the decree or that the separation had ceased or been discontinued.*

Note. Repealed by Matrimonial Causes Act 1950, Schedule.

For former statutory provisions, see Matrimonial Causes Act 1858, ss 8, 10 (pp 2015, 2016).

196. Power to vary orders. *The court may from time to time vary or modify any order for the periodical payment of money made under the provisions of this Act relating to matrimonial causes and matters either by altering the times of payment or by increasing or diminishing the amount, or may temporarily suspend the order as to the whole or any part of the money ordered to be paid, and subsequently revive it wholly or in part, as the court thinks just.*

Note. Repealed by Administration of Justice (Miscellaneous Provisions) Act 1938, s 20, Sch 4. See now Matrimonial Causes Act 1973, s 31 (p 2503), replacing Matrimonial Proceedings and Property Act 1970, s 9 (p 2350), replacing Matrimonial Causes Act 1965, s 31 (p 2241), replacing Matrimonial Causes Act 1950, s 28 (p 2132), replacing Administration of Justice (Miscellaneous Provisions) Act 1938, s 14.

For former statutory provision, see Matrimonial Causes Act 1884, s 4 (p 2033).

197. Power to allow intervention on terms. *In every case in which any person is charged with adultery with any party to a suit or in which the court may consider, in the interest of any person not already a party to the suit, that that person should be made a party to the suit, the court may, if it thinks fit, allow that person to intervene upon such terms, if any, as the court thinks just.*

Note. Repealed by Matrimonial Causes Act 1950, s 34(1), Schedule. See now Matrimonial Causes Act 1973, s 49(5) (p 2523), replacing Matrimonial Causes Act 1965, s 44 (p 2249), replacing Matrimonial Causes Act 1950, s 31 (p 2133).

For former statutory provision, see Matrimonial Causes Act 1907, s 3 (p 2035).

198. Evidence. *The parties to any proceedings instituted in consequence of adultery and the husbands and wives of the parties shall be competent to give evidence in the proceedings, but no witness in any such proceedings, whether a party thereto or not, shall be liable to be asked or be bound to answer any question tending to show that he or she has been guilty of adultery unless he or she has already given evidence in the same proceedings in disproof of the alleged adultery.*

Note. Repealed by Matrimonial Causes Act 1950, s 34(1), Schedule, replaced by ibid, s 32(3) (p 2154), replaced by Matrimonial Causes Act 1965, s 43(2) (p 2248) which was repealed by Matrimonial Causes Act 1973, s 54(1), Sch 3, and not replaced.

[**198A.** *In any proceedings for nullity of marriage, evidence on the question of sexual capacity shall be heard in camera unless in any case the judge is satisfied that in the interests of justice any such evidence ought to be heard in open court.*]

Note. Section 198A added by Supreme Court of Judicature (Amendment) Act 1935, s 4, and repealed and re-enacted by Matrimonial Causes Act 1950 (see ibid, s 32(4), p 2133), replaced by Matrimonial Causes Act 1965, s 43(3) (p 2248), and now replaced by Matrimonial Causes Act 1973, s 48(2) (p 2522).

199. Power of Secretary of State to order records to be transmitted from ecclesiastical courts—(*1*) *A Secretary of State may order any judge, registrar or other officer of any ecclesiastical court in England or the Isle of Man, or any other person having the public custody or control of any records, books, documents or other instruments relating to matrimonial causes and matters to transmit the same at such times, and in such manner, and to such places in London or Westminster, and subject to such regulations, as the Secretary of State may appoint.*

(*2*) *If any person wilfully disobeys an order made under this section he shall for the first offence forfeit the sum of one hundred pounds to be recoverable as a debt in the court by any registrar of the principal probate registry, and for a second or any subsequent offence the court may, by a warrant of committal countersigned by a Secretary of State, commit the person so offending to prison for any period not exceeding three months.*

Note. For former statutory provision, see Matrimonial Causes Act 1857, s 66 (p 2013).

Repealed by Public Records Act 1958, Sch 4: see now para 4(1)(n) of the First Schedule to that Act, which makes the records of the ecclesiastical courts, when exercising testamentary and matrimonial jurisdiction, 'public records'.

200. Seal of court for use in matrimonial causes—(*1*) *The seal of the court to be used in respect of its jurisdiction in matrimonial causes and matters shall be such as the Lord Chancellor may from time to time direct.*

(*2*) *All decrees and orders of the court, or copies thereof, made in pursuance of the said jurisdiction shall, if purporting to be sealed with the said seal, be received in evidence in all parts in the United Kingdom without further proof.*

Note. For former statutory provision, see Matrimonial Causes Act 1857, s 13 (p 2003).

*　　*　　*　　*　　*

SCHEDULES

FIRST SCHEDULE   Section 99

ENACTMENTS CONTAINING AND REGULATING MATTERS WITH RESPECT TO WHICH RULES OF COURT MAY BE MADE

Session and Chapter	Title or Short Title	Enactments affected
*　*　*	*　*　*	*　*　*
20 & 21 Vict c 85.	The Matrimonial Causes Act 1857.	Sections thirty-nine, forty-one to forty-four, forty-six and forty-nine.
21 & 22 Vict c 93.	The Legitimacy Declaration Act 1858.	Section three.
*　*　*	*　*　*	*　*　*
21 & 22 Vict c 108.	The Matrimonial Causes Act 1858.	Section thirteen.
*　*　*	*　*　*	*　*　*

Note. This Schedule repealed by Supreme Court Act 1981, s 152(4), Sch 7.

SIXTH SCHEDULE

Session and Chapter	Title or Short Title	Enactments affected
*　*　*	*　*　*	*　*　*
20 & 21 Vict c 85.	The Matrimonial Causes Act 1857.	Sections two, six, seven, twelve, thirteen, sixteen and seventeen,

Session and Chapter	Title or Short Title	Enactments affected
		and so far as it relates to the High Court section twenty-one, sections twenty-two to thirty-one, thirty-three to thirty-five, forty-five, fifty-five, fifty-seven, fifty-eight and sixty-six.
* * *	* * *	* * *
20 & 22 Vict c 93.	*The Legitimacy Declaration Act 1858.*	*The whole Act, except section three and except so far as the Act relates to Scotland.*
* * *	* * *	* * *
21 & 22 Vict c 108.	*The Matrimonial Causes Act 1858.*	*Sections four, six to eleven, and fifteen.*
* * *	* * *	* * *
22 & 23 Vict c 61.	*The Matrimonial Causes Act 1859.*	*The whole Act.*
* * *	* * *	* * *
23 & 24 Vict c 144.	*The Matrimonial Causes Act 1860.*	*The whole Act.*
* * *	* * *	* * *
27 & 28 Vict c 44.	*The Matrimonial Causes Act 1864.*	*The whole Act so far as it relates to the High Court.*
* * *	* * *	* * *
29 & 30 Vict c 22.	*The Matrimonial Causes Act 1866.*	*The whole Act.*
31 & 32 Vict c 77.	*The Matrimonial Causes Act 1868.*	*The whole Act.*
32 & 33 Vict c 68.	*The Evidence Further Amendment Act 1869.*	*Section three so far as it relates to the High Court.*
* * *	* * *	* * *
36 & 37 Vict c 31.	*The Matrimonial Causes Act 1873.*	*The whole Act.*
* * *	* * *	* * *
41 & 42 Vict c 19.	*The Matrimonial Causes Act 1878.*	*The whole Act.*
* * *	* * *	* * *
44 & 45 Vict c 68.	*The Supreme Court of Judicature Act 1881.*	*The whole Act except section one and the third and fourth paragraphs of section 9.*
* * *	* * *	* * *
47 & 48 Vict c 68.	*The Matrimonial Causes Act 1884.*	*The whole Act.*
* * *	* * *	* * *
7 Edw 7 c 12.	*The Matrimonial Causes Act 1907.*	*The whole Act.*
* * *	* * *	* * *
13 & 14 Geo 5 c 19.	*The Matrimonial Causes Act 1923.*	*The whole Act.*
* * *	* * *	* * *

Note. This Schedule repealed by Statute Law Revision Act 1950.

JUDICIAL PROCEEDINGS (REGULATION OF REPORTS) ACT 1926

(16 & 17 Geo 5 c 61)

An Act to regulate the publication of reports of judicial proceedings in such manner as to prevent injury to public morals. [15 December 1926]

1. Restriction on publication of reports of judicial proceedings—(1) It shall not be lawful to print or publish, or cause or procure to be printed or published—

    (a) in relation to any judicial proceedings any indecent matter or indecent medical, surgical or physiological details being matter or details the publication of which would be calculated to injure public morals;

    (b) in relation to [any proceedings under Part II of the Family Law Act 1996 or otherwise in relation to] any judicial proceedings for dissolution of marriage, for nullity of marriage, or for judicial separation, or for restitution of conjugal rights, any particulars other than the following, that is to say—

        (i) the names, addresses and occupations of the parties and witnesses;

        (ii) a concise statement of the charges, defences and countercharges in support of which evidence has been given;

        (iii) submissions on any point of law arising in the course of the proceedings, and the decision of the court thereon;

        (iv) the summing-up of the judge and the finding of the jury (if any) and the judgment of the court and observations made by the judge in giving judgment:

Provided that nothing in this part of this subsection shall be held to permit the publication of anything contrary to the provisions of paragraph (a) of this subsection.

Note. Sub-s (1)(b) extended and modified by Domestic and Appellate Proceedings (Restriction of Publicity) Act 1968, s 2(3) (p 2266). Words in square brackets in sub-s (1)(b) inserted by Family Law Act 1996, s 66(1), Sch 8, Part I, para 2, as from a day to be appointed, subject to savings in s 66(2) of, and para 5 of Sch 9 to, the 1996 Act.

(2) If any person acts in contravention of the provisions of this Act, he shall in respect of each offence be liable, on summary conviction, to imprisonment for a term not exceeding four months, or to a fine not exceeding *five hundred pounds* [level 5 on standard scale], or to both such imprisonment and fine:

Provided that no person, other than a proprietor, editor, master printer or publisher, shall be liable to be convicted under this Act.

Note. Reference to level 5 effected by Criminal Justice Act 1982, ss 37, 38(1), (6), 46(1).

(3) No prosecution for an offence under this Act shall be commenced in England and Wales by any person without the sanction of the Attorney-General.

(4) Nothing in this section shall apply to the printing of any pleading, transcript of evidence or other document for use in connection with any judicial proceedings or the communication thereof to persons concerned in the proceedings, or to the printing or publishing of any notice or report in pursuance of the directions of the court; or to the printing or publishing of any matter in any separate volume or part of any bonâ fide series of law reports which does not form part of any other publication and consists solely of reports of proceedings in courts of law, or in any publication of a technical character bonâ fide intended for circulation among members of the legal or medical professions.

(5) [Application to Scotland.]

Note. Cf Magistrates' Courts Act 1980, s 71 (p 2730); and see Administration of Justice Act 1960, s 12 (p 2213), as to publication of information relating to proceedings in private.

2. Short title and extent—(1) This Act may be cited as the Judicial Proceedings (Regulation of Reports) Act 1926.

(2) This Act does not extend to Northern Ireland.

EVIDENCE (FOREIGN, DOMINION AND COLONIAL DOCUMENTS) ACT 1933

(23 & 24 Geo 5 c 4)

An Act to make further and better provision with respect to the admissibility in evidence in the United Kingdom of entries contained in the public registers of other countries and with respect to the proof by means of duly authenticated official certificates of entries in such registers and in consular registers and of other matters. [29 March 1933]

1. *Proof and effect of foreign, dominion and colonial registers and certain official certificates—* (*1*) *If, upon consideration of a report from the Lord Chancellor and a Secretary of State, His Majesty in Council is satisfied with respect to any country that, having regard to the law of that country as to the recognition therein of public registers of the United Kingdom as authentic records and as to the proof of the contents of such registers and other matters by means of duly authenticated certificates issued by public officers in the United Kingdom, it is desirable in the interests of reciprocity to make with respect to public registers of that country and certificates issued by public officers therein such an Order as is hereinafter mentioned, it shall be lawful for His Majesty in Council to make such an Order accordingly.**

(2) An Order in Council made under *this section* [section 5 of the Oaths and Evidence (Overseas Authorities and Countries) Act 1963] may provide that in all parts of the United Kingdom—

(a) a register of the country to which the Order relates, being such a register as is specified in the Order, shall be deemed to be a public register kept under the authority of the law of that country and recognised by the courts thereof as an authentic record, and to be a document of such a public nature as to be admissible as evidence of the matters regularly recorded therein;

(b) such matters as may be specified in the Order shall, if recorded in such a register, be deemed, until the contrary is proved, to be regularly recorded therein;

(c) subject to any conditions specified in the Order and to any requirements of rules of court a document purporting to be issued in the country to which the Order relates as an official copy of an entry in such a register as is so specified, and purporting to be authenticated as such in the manner specified in the Order as appropriate in the case of such a register, shall, without evidence as to the custody of the register or of inability to produce it and without any further or other proof, be received as evidence that the register contains such an entry;

(d) subject as aforesaid a certificate purporting to be given in the country to which the Order relates as an official certificate of any such class as is specified in the Order, and purporting to be signed by the officer, and to be authenticated in

---

* The following Orders have been made: SR & O 1933 No 383 (Belgium); 1937 No 515 (France); 1938 No 739 (Australia); 1959 No 1306 (New Zealand); 1961 Nos 2041–2053 (Bahamas, Bermuda, British Guiana, British Honduras, Dominica, Fiji, Gibraltar, Mauritius, St Helena, Sarawak, Tanganyika, Uganda, Zanzibar); 1962 Nos 641–644 (Barbados, Hong Kong, Jamaica, Montserrat); 1962 Nos 2605–2609 (British Antarctic Territory, certain provinces of Canada, Falkland Islands, Seychelles, Sierra Leone); Guernsey (SI 1973 No 610); Isle of Man (SI 1973 No 611); Jersey (SI 1973 No 612); Italy (SI 1973 No 1894); Tonga (SI 1980 No 1523); and Surinam (SI 1981 No 735). SI 1933 No 1073 is amended by Zimbabwe (Independence and Membership of Commonwealth) (Consequential Provisions) Order 1980, SI 1980 No 701, art 7, Schedule, para 4(1). The validity of these Orders is not affected by the repeal of s 1(1): Oaths and Evidence (Overseas Authorities and Countries) Act 1963, s 5(2). See Appendix II (p 2217), where the requirements of the various Orders are set out. For Orders made under Oaths and Evidence (Overseas Authorities and Countries) Act 1963, s 5: see footnote on p 2217.

the manner, specified in the Order as appropriate in the case of a certificate of that class, shall be received as evidence of the facts stated in the certificate;

(e) no official document issued in the country to which the Order relates as proof of any matters for the proof of which provision is made by the Order shall, if otherwise admissible in evidence, be inadmissible by reason only that it is not authenticated by the process known as legislation.

(3) Official books of record preserved in a central registry and containing entries copied from original registers may, if those entries were copied by officials in the course of their duty, themselves be treated for the purposes of this section as registers.

(4) In this section the expression 'country' means a Dominion, the Isle of Man, any of the Channel Islands, a British colony or protectorate, a foreign country, a colony or protectorate of a foreign country, or any mandated territory:

Provided that where a part of a country is under both a local and a central legislature, an Order under this section may be made as well with respect to that part, as with respect to all the parts under that central legislature.

(5) *His Majesty in Council may vary or revoke any Order previously made under this section.*

Note. Sub-ss (1), (5) repealed and words in square brackets in sub-s (2) substituted for words in italics by Oaths and Evidence (Overseas Authorities and Countries) Act 1963, s 5.

*   *   *   *   *

3. Short title. This Act may be cited as the Evidence (Foreign, Dominion and Colonial Documents) Act 1933.

CHILDREN AND YOUNG PERSONS ACT 1933

(23 & 24 Geo 5 c 12)

An Act to consolidate certain enactments relating to persons under the age of eighteen years.   [13 April 1933]

*   *   *   *   *

36. Prohibition against children being present in court during trial of other persons. No child (other than an infant in arms) shall be permitted to be present in court during the trial of any other person charged with an offence, or during any proceedings preliminary thereto, except during such time as his presence is required as a witness or otherwise for the purposes of justice; and any child present in court when under this section he is not to be permitted to be so shall be ordered to be removed:

Provided that this section shall not apply to messengers, clerks, and other persons required to attend at any court for purposes connected with their employment.

37. Power to clear court while child or young person is giving evidence in certain cases—(1) Where, in any proceedings in relation to an offence against, or any conduct contrary to, decency or morality, a person who, in the opinion of the court is a child or young person is called as a witness, the court may direct that all or any persons, not being members or officers of the court or parties to the case, their counsel or solicitors, or persons otherwise directly concerned with the case, be excluded from the court during the taking of the evidence of that witness:

Provided that nothing in this section shall authorise the exclusion of bona fide representatives of a newspaper or news agency.

(2) The powers conferred on a court by this section shall be in addition and without prejudice to any other powers of the court to hear proceedings in camera.

38. Evidence of child of tender years—(*1*) *Where, in any proceedings against any person for any offence, any child of tender years called as a witness does not in the opinion of* *the court understand the nature of an oath, his evidence may be received, though not given upon oath, if, in the opinion of the court, he is possessed of sufficient intelligence to justify the reception of the evidence, and understands the duty of speaking the truth; and his evidence, though not given on oath, but otherwise taken and reduced into writing in accordance with the provisions of section seventeen of the Indictable Offences Act 1848, or of this Part of this Act, shall be deemed to be a deposition within the meaning of that section and that Part respectively:*

Provided that where evidence admitted by virtue of this section is given on behalf of the prosecution the accused shall not be liable to be convicted of the offence unless that evidence is corroborated by some other material evidence in support thereof implicating him.

(2) If any child whose evidence is received *as aforesaid* [unsworn in any proceedings for an offence by virtue of section 52 of the Criminal Justice Act 1991] wilfully gives false evidence in such circumstances that he would, if the evidence had been given on oath, have been guilty of perjury, he shall be liable on summary conviction to be dealt with as if he had been summarily convicted of an indictable offence punishable in the case of an adult with imprisonment.

Note. Sub-s (1) repealed by Criminal Justice Act 1991, s 101(2), Sch 13, as from 1 October 1992. Proviso to sub-s (1) repealed by Criminal Justice Act 1988, ss 34(1), 170(2), Sch 16, except in relation to proceedings before a magistrates' court acting as examining justices, or to a trial, which began before 12 October 1988. Words in square brackets in sub-s (2) substituted for words in italics by Criminal Justice Act 1991, s 100, Sch 11, para 1, as from 1 October 1992.

39. Power to prohibit publication of certain matter in newspapers—(1) In relation to any proceedings in any court ... the court may direct that—

(a) no newspaper report of the proceedings shall reveal the name, address, or school, or include any particulars calculated to lead to the identification, of any child or young person concerned in the proceedings, either as being the person [by or against] or in respect of whom the proceedings are taken, or as being a witness therein;

(b) no picture shall be published in any newspaper as being or including a picture of any child or young person so concerned in the proceedings as aforesaid;

except in so far (if at all) as may be permitted by the direction of the court.

(2) Any person who publishes any matter in contravention of any such direction shall on summary conviction be liable in respect of each offence to a fine not exceeding £500 [level 5 on the standard scale].

Note. In sub-s (1) words omitted repealed by Children and Young Persons Act 1963, ss 57(1), 64(3), Sch 5, and words in square brackets substituted by s 57(1) of that Act. Reference to level 5 substituted by virtue of Criminal Justice Act 1982, ss 39, 46, Sch 3.

Special Procedure with regard to Offences specified in First Schedule

40. Warrant to search for or remove a child or young person—*(1) If it appears to a justice of the peace on information on oath laid by any person who, in the opinion of the justice, is acting in the interests of a child or young person, that there is reasonable cause to suspect—*

(a) that the child or young person has been or is being assaulted, ill-treated, or neglected in any place within the jurisdiction of the justice, in a manner likely to cause him unnecessary suffering, or injury to health; or

(b) that any offence mentioned in the First Schedule to this Act has been or is being committed in respect of the child or young person,

the justice may issue a warrant authorising any constable named therein to search for the child or young person, and, if it is found that he has been or is being assaulted, ill-treated, or neglected in manner aforesaid, or that any such offence as aforesaid has been or is being committed in respect of him [to take him to a place of safety, or authorising any constable to remove him with or without search to a place of safety, and a child or young person taken to a place of safety in pursuance of such a warrant may be detained there] until he can be brought before a juvenile court.

(2) A justice issuing a warrant under this section may by the same warrant cause any person accused of any offence in respect of the child or young person to be apprehended and brought before a court of summary jurisdiction, and proceedings to be taken against him according to law.

(*3*) *Any constable authorised by warrant under this section to search for any child or young person, or to remove any child or young person with or without search, may enter (if need be by force) any house, building, or other place specified in the warrant, and may remove him therefrom.*

(*4*) *Every warrant issued under this section shall be addressed to and executed by a constable, who shall be accompanied by the person laying the information, if that person so desires, unless the justice by whom the warrant is issued otherwise directs, and may also, if the justice by whom the warrant is issued so directs, be accompanied by a duly qualified medical practitioner.*

(*5*) *It shall not be necessary in any information or warrant under this section to name the child or young person.*

Note. This section repealed by Children Act 1989, s 108(4), (7), Sch 12, para 3, Sch 15, as from 14 October 1991. For transitional provisions, see Sch 14, paras 1, 27, to that Act (pp 3373, 3384). Words 'named herein' in sub-s (1) and words 'addressed to and' in sub-s (4) repealed by Police and Criminal Evidence Act 1984, s 119(2), Sch 7, Part I. Words in square brackets in sub-s (1) substituted by Children and Young Persons Act 1963, s 64(1), Sch 3, para 11.

41. Power to proceed with case in absence of child or young person. Where in any proceedings with relation to any of the offences mentioned in the First Schedule to this Act, the court is satisfied that the attendance before the court of any child or young person in respect of whom the offence is alleged to have been committed is not essential to the just hearing of the case, the case may be proceeded with and determined in the absence of the child or young person.

42. Extension of power to take deposition of child or young person—(1) Where a justice of the peace is satisfied by the evidence of a duly qualified medical practitioner that the attendance before the court of any child or young person in respect of whom any of the offences mentioned in the First Schedule to this Act is alleged to have been committed would involve serious danger to his life or health, the justice may take in writing the deposition of the child or young person on oath, and shall thereupon subscribe the deposition and add thereto a statement of his reason for taking it and of the day when and place where it was taken, and of the names of the persons (if any) present at the taking thereof.

(2) The justice taking any such deposition shall transmit it with his statement—

(a) if the deposition relates to an offence for which any accused person is already committed for trial, to the proper officer of the court for trial at which the accused person has been committed; and

(b) in any other case, to the clerk of the court before which proceedings are pending in respect of the offence.

43. Admission of deposition of child or young person in evidence. Where, in any proceedings in respect of any of the offences mentioned in the First Schedule to this Act, the court is satisfied by the evidence of a duly qualified medical practitioner that the attendance before the court of any child or young person in respect of whom the offence is alleged to have been committed would involve serious danger to his life or health, any deposition of the child or young person taken under the Indictable Offences Act 1848, or this Part of this Act, shall be admissible in evidence either for or against the accused person without further proof thereof if it purports to be signed by the justice by or before whom it purports to be taken:

Provided that the deposition shall not be admissible in evidence against the accused person unless it is proved that reasonable notice of the intention to take the deposition has been served upon him and that he or his counsel or solicitor had, or might have had if he had chosen to be present, an opportunity of cross-examining the child or young person making the deposition.

Principles to be observed by all Courts in dealing with Children and Young Persons

44. General considerations—(1) Every court in dealing with a child or young person who is brought before it, either as ... an offender or otherwise, shall have regard to the welfare of the child or young person and shall in a proper case take steps for removing him from undesirable surroundings, and for securing proper provision is made for his education and training.

(2) ...

Note. Words omitted from sub-s (1) and whole of sub-s (2) repealed by Children and Young Persons Act 1969, s 72(4), Sch 6. Children Act 1989, s 1 (p 3205) provides that when a court determines any question with respect to the upbringing of a child or the administration of a child's property or the application of any income arising from it, the child's welfare shall be the court's paramount consideration.

Juvenile Courts

45. Constitution of juvenile courts. Courts of summary jurisdiction constituted in accordance with the provisions of the Second Schedule to this Act and sitting for the purpose of hearing any charge against a child or young person or for the purpose of exercising any other jurisdiction conferred on *juvenile courts* [youth courts] by or under this or any other Act, shall be known as *juvenile courts* [youth courts] and in whatever place sitting shall be deemed to be petty sessional courts.

Note. Words in square brackets substituted for words in italics by Criminal Justice Act 1991, s 100, Sch 11, para 40(1), (2)(a), as from 1 October 1991.

*   *   *   *   *

49. Restrictions on newspaper reports of proceedings in juvenile courts— (*1*) *Subject as hereinafter provided, no newspaper report of any proceedings in a juvenile court shall reveal the name, address or school, or include any particulars calculated to lead to the identification, of any child or young person concerned in those proceedings, either as being the person against or in respect of whom the proceedings are taken or as being a witness therein, nor shall any picture be published in any newspaper as being or including a picture of any child or young person so concerned in any such proceedings as aforesaid:*

Provided that the court or the Secretary of State may in any case, if satisfied that it is [*appropriate to do so for the purpose of avoiding injustice to a child or young person*], *by order dispense with the requirements of this section* [*in relation to him*] *to such extent as may be specified in the order.*

(*2*) *Any person who publishes any matter in contravention of this section shall on summary conviction be liable in respect of each offence to a fine not exceeding £500* [*level 5 on the standard scale*].

Note. Words in square brackets in sub-s (1) substituted and inserted, respectively, by Children and Young Persons Act 1969, s 10(1). In sub-s (2) reference to level 5 substituted by virtue of Criminal Justice Act 1982, ss 39, 46, Sch 3. Fine previously increased to £500 by Criminal Law Act 1977, s 31, Sch 6.

[**49. Restrictions on reports of proceedings in which children or young persons are concerned**—(1) The following prohibitions apply (subject to subsection (5) below) in relation to any proceedings to which this section applies, that is to say—

    (a) no report shall be published which reveals the name, address or school of any child or young person concerned in the proceedings or includes any particulars likely to lead to the identification of any child or young person concerned in the proceedings; and

    (b) no picture shall be published or included in a programme service as being or including a picture of any child or young person concerned in the proceedings.

    (2) The proceedings to which this section applies are—

    (a) proceedings in a youth court;

    (b) proceedings on appeal from a youth court (including proceedings by way of case stated);

(c) proceedings under section 15 or 16 of the Children and Young Persons Act 1969 (proceedings for varying or revoking supervision orders); and

(d) proceedings on appeal from a magistrates' court arising out of proceedings under section 15 or 16 of that Act (including proceedings by way of case stated).

(3) The reports to which this section applies are reports in a newspaper and reports included in a programme service; and similarly as respects pictures.

(4) For the purposes of this section a child or young person is 'concerned' in any proceedings whether as being the person against or in respect of whom the proceedings are taken or as being a witness in the proceedings.

(5) Subject to subsection (7) below, a court may, in relation to proceedings before it to which this section applies, by order dispense to any specified extent with the requirements of this section in relation to a child or young person who is concerned in the proceedings if it is satisfied—

(a) that it is appropriate to do so for the purpose of avoiding injustice to the child or young person; or

(b) that, as respects a child or young person to whom this paragraph applies who is unlawfully at large, it is necessary to dispense with those requirements for the purpose of apprehending him and bringing him before a court or returning him to the place in which he was in custody.

(6) Paragraph (b) of subsection (5) above applies to any child or young person who is charged with or has been convicted of—

(a) a violent offence,

(b) a sexual offence,

(c) an offence punishable in the case of a person aged 21 or over with imprisonment for fourteen years or more.

(7) The court shall not exercise its power under subsection (5)(b) above—

(a) except in pursuance of an application by or on behalf of the Director of Public Prosecutions; and

(b) unless notice of the application has been given by the Director of Public Prosecutions to any legal representative of the child or young person.

(8) The court's power under subsection (5) above may be exercised by a single justice.

(9) If a report or picture is published or included in a programme service in contravention of subsection (1) above, the following persons, that is to say—

(a) in the case of publication of a written report or a picture as part of a newspaper, any proprietor, editor or publisher of the newspaper;

(b) in the case of the inclusion of a report or picture in a programme service, any body corporate which provides the service and any person having functions in relation to the programme corresponding to those of an editor of a newspaper, shall be liable on summary conviction to a fine not exceeding level 5 on the standard scale.

(10) In any proceedings under section 15 or 16 of the Children and Young Persons Act 1969 (proceedings for varying or revoking supervision orders) before a magistrates' court other than a youth court or on appeal from such a court it shall be the duty of the magistrates' court or the appellate court to announce in the course of the proceedings that this section applies to the proceedings; and if the court fails to do so this section shall not apply to the proceedings.

(11) In this section—

'legal representative' means an authorised advocate or authorised litigator, as defined by section 119(1) of the Courts and Legal Services Act 1990;

'programme' and 'programme service' have the same meaning as in the Broadcasting Act 1990;

'sexual offence' has the same meaning as in section 31(1) of the Criminal Justice Act 1991;

'specified' means specified in an order under this section;
'violent offence' has the same meaning as in section 31(1) of the Criminal
   Justice Act 1991;
and a person who, having been granted bail, is liable to arrest (whether with or
without a warrant) shall be treated as unlawfully at large.]

Note. Section 49 in square brackets substituted for s 49 in italics by Criminal Justice and
Public Order Act 1994, s 49, as from 3 February 1995.

Juvenile Offenders

50. Age of criminal responsibility. It shall be conclusively presumed that no
child under the age of [ten] years can be guilty of any offence.

Note. Word in square brackets substituted by Children and Young Persons Act 1963, s 16(1).
   Section as originally enacted provided that it should be conclusively presumed that no
child under the age of eight could be guilty of any offence, thereby raising the then age of
criminal responsibility by one year.
   A similar presumption exists in the case of sexual and unnatural offences by boys under
the age of fourteen years. In the case of other crimes by an infant between the ages of ten
and fourteen years the presumption of incapacity may be rebutted.
   Under Children and Young Persons Act 1963, s 16(2) in any proceedings for an offence
committed by a person of or over the age of twenty-one any offence of which he was found
guilty while under fourteen is to be disregarded for the purposes of any evidence relating to
his previous convictions.

* * * * *

PART VI SUPPLEMENTAL

Local Authorities

96. Provisions as to local authorities—(1) Subject to the modifications hereinafter contained as to the City of London, where any powers or duties are by [Part II
of this Act] conferred or imposed on local authorities (by that description), those
powers and duties shall ... be powers and duties of local education authorities ...
   [(1A) The local authorities for the purposes of Parts III and IV of this Act shall
be the councils of counties (other than metropolitan counties), of metropolitan
districts and of London boroughs and the Common Council of the City of London
[but, in relation to Wales, shall be the councils of counties and county boroughs].]
   (2) ...
   (3) Expenses incurred by a local authority in connection with powers and duties
which are, under this Act, exercised and performed by them as local education
authorities [shall be defrayed as expenses under the enactments relating to
education].
   (4) Expenses incurred under this Act by the council of a county or county
borough, exclusive of any expenses to be defrayed [in accordance with] the last
foregoing subsection ... shall be defrayed—
   (a) ...
   (b) ... as expenses for general county purposes or, as the case may be, out of
       the general rate.
   [(4A) Subsection (4) does not apply in relation to the council of any Welsh
county or county borough.]
   (5), (6) ...
   (7) [Subject to the provisions of [sections 2 and 3 of the Local Authority Social
Services Act 1970 (which require certain matters to be referred to the social services
committee and restrict the reference of other matters to that committee)]] a local
authority may refer to a committee appointed for the purposes of this Act, or to any
committee appointed for the purposes of any other Act, any matter relating to the
exercise by the authority of any of their powers under this Act and may delegate any
of the said powers (other than any power to borrow money) to any such committee.

(8) A local authority, or a committee to whom any powers of a local authority under this Act have been delegated, may by resolution empower the clerk or the chief education officer of the authority to exercise in the name of the authority in any case which appears to him to be one of urgency any powers of the authority or, as the case may be, of the committee with respect to the institution of proceedings under this Act.

Note. In sub-s (1) words in square brackets substituted by Children Act 1948, s 60(2), Sch 3, and words omitted repealed by Education Act 1944, s 121, Sch 9, Part I.

Sub-s (1A) inserted by Child Care Act 1980, s 89(2), Sch 5, para 1; sub-s (2) repealed and words in square brackets in sub-s (3) substituted by Education Act 1944, s 120, Sch 8, Part I.

Words in square brackets in sub-s (1A), and sub-s (4A), added by Local Government (Wales) Act 1994, s 22(4), Sch 10, para 1, as from 1 April 1996.

In sub-s (4) words in square brackets substituted by Education Act 1944, s 120, Sch 8, Part I; words omitted in the first place repealed by Education Act 1944, s 121, Sch 9, Part I, and in the second and third places by National Assistance Act 1948, s 62, Sch 7, Part III.

Sub-s (5) repealed by Acquisition of Land Act 1981, s 34(3), Sch 6, Part II, and sub-s (6) repealed by London Government Act 1963, s 93(1), Sch 18, Part II.

In sub-s (7) words from 'Subject to' to 'that committee' originally inserted by Children Act 1948, s 60(2), Sch 3, further amended by Local Authority Social Services Act 1970, s 14, Sch 2, para 1.

*   *   *   *   *

Supplementary Provisions as to Legal Proceedings

99. Presumption and determination of age—(1) Where a person, whether charged with an offence or not, is brought before any court otherwise than for the purpose of giving evidence, and it appears to the court that he is a child or young person, the court shall make due inquiry as to the age of that person, and for that purpose shall take such evidence as may be forthcoming at the hearing of the case, but an order or judgment of the court shall not be invalidated by any subsequent proof that the age of that person has not been correctly stated to the court, and the age presumed or declared by the court to be the age of the person so brought before it shall, for the purposes of this Act, be deemed to be the true age of that person, and, where it appears to the court that the person so brought before it has attained *the age of seventeen* [the age of eighteen] years, that person shall for the purposes of this Act be deemed not be be a child or young person.

(2) Where in any charge or indictment for any offence under this Act or any of the offences mentioned in the First Schedule to this Act, [except as provided in that Schedule], it is alleged that the person by or in respect of whom the offence was committed was a child or young person or was under or had attained any specified age, and he appears to the court to have been at the date of the commission of the alleged offence a child or young person, or to have been under or to have attained the specified age, as the case may be, he shall for the purposes of this Act be presumed at that date to have been a child or young person or to have been under or to have attained that age, as the case may be, unless the contrary is proved.

(3) Where, in any charge or indictment for any offence under this Act or any of the offences mentioned in the First Schedule to this Act, it is alleged that the person in respect of whom the offence was committed was a child or was a young person, it shall not be a defence to prove that the person alleged to have been a child was a young person or the person alleged to have been a young person was a child in any case where the acts constituting the alleged offence would equally have been an offence if committed in respect of a young person or child respectively.

(4) Where a person is charged with an offence under this Act in respect of a person apparently under a specified age it shall be a defence to prove that the person was actually of or over that age.

Note. Words in square brackets in sub-s (1) substituted for words in italics by Criminal Justice Act 1991, s 68, Sch 8, para 1(2), as from 1 October 1992. Words in square brackets in sub-s (2) substituted by Sexual Offences Act 1956, s 48, Sch 3.

* * * * *

101. Application of Summary Jurisdiction Acts—(1) Subject to the provisions of this Act, all orders of a court of summary jurisdiction, whether a petty sessional court or not, under this Act shall be made, and all proceedings in relation to any such orders shall be taken, in manner provided by the Summary Jurisdiction Acts ...

(2) ...

Note. Words omitted from sub-s (1) and whole of sub-s (2) repealed by Justices of the Peace Act 1949, s 46(2), Sch 7, Part II. See now Magistrates' Courts Act 1980 (p 2714).

* * * * *

107. Interpretation—(1) In this Act, unless the context otherwise requires, the following expressions have the meanings hereby respectively assigned to them, that is to say,—

* * * * *

[*'Care order' and 'interim order' have the same meanings as in the Children and Young Persons Act 1969;*]

'Chief officer of police' [*as regards England has the same meaning as in the Police Act 1964*], as regards Scotland has the same meaning as in [the Police (Scotland) Act 1967], and as regards Northern Ireland means a district inspector of the Royal Ulster Constabulary;

'Child' means a person under the age of fourteen years;

'Guardian', in relation to a child or young person, includes any person who, in the opinion of the court having cognisance of any case in relation to the child or young person or in which the child or young person is concerned, has for the time being the *charge of or control over* [care of] the child or young person;

* * * * *

'Intoxicating liquor' [has the same meaning as in the Licensing Act 1964];

'Legal guardian' in relation to a child or young person, means a person appointed, according to law, to be his guardian by deed or will, or by order of a court of competent jurisdiction;

['Legal guardian', in relation to a child or young person, means a guardian of a child as defined in the Children Act 1989;]

* * * * *

'Place of safety' means [a community home provided by a local authority or a controlled community home] any police station, or any hospital, surgery, or any other suitable place, the occupier of which is willing temporarily to receive a child or young person;

* * * * *

'Prescribed' means prescribed by regulations made by the Secretary of State;

'Public place' includes any public park, garden, sea beach or railway station, and any ground to which the public for the time being have or are permitted to have access, whether on payment or otherwise;

* * * * *

'Street' includes any highway and any public bridge, road, lane, footway, square, court, alley or passage, whether a thoroughfare or not;

'*Young person' means a person who has attained the age of fourteen years and is under the age of seventeen years.*

['Young person' means a person who has attained the age of fourteen and is under the age of eighteen years.]

(2) ...

(3) References in this Act to any enactment or to any provision in any enactment shall, unless the context otherwise requires, be construed as references to that enactment or provision as amended by any subsequent enactment including this Act.

Note. Definitions omitted from sub-s (1) repealed by National Assistance Act 1948, s 62, Sch 7, Part III; Children and Young Persons Act 1963, s 64(3), Sch 5; Police Act 1964, s 64(3), Sch 10; Children and Young Persons Act 1969, s 72(4), Sch 6; Child Care Act 1980, s 89(3), Sch 6; and Statute Law (Repeals) Act 1986.

Definitions 'care order' and 'interim order' inserted by Children and Young Persons Act 1969, s 72(3), Sch 5, para 12, repealed by Children Act 1989, s 108(7), Sch 15, as from 14 October 1991; in the definition 'chief officer of police' the words in the first square brackets substituted by Police Act 1964, s 63, Sch 9, repealed by Police Act 1996, s 103(3), Sch 9, Part I, as from 22 August 1996, and words in second square brackets substituted by Police (Scotland) Act 1967, ss 52, 53, Sch 4; words in square brackets in definition 'guardian' substituted for words in italics, and definition 'legal guardian' in square brackets substituted for that definition in italics by Children Act 1989, s 108(5), Sch 13, para 7, as from 14 October 1991; words in square brackets in definition 'intoxicating liquor' substituted by Finance Act 1967, s 5(1)(e); and words in square brackets in the definition 'place of safety' substituted by Children and Young Persons Act 1969, s 72(3), Sch 5, para 12. Definition 'young person' in square brackets substituted for that definition in italics by Criminal Justice Act 1991, s 68, Sch 8, para 1(3), as from 1 October 1992.

Sub-s (2) repealed by Children and Young Persons Act 1969, s 72(3), (4), Sch 5, para 12, Sch 6.

*   *   *   *   *

109. Short title, commencement, extent and repeals—(1) This Act may be cited as the Children and Young Persons Act 1933.

FOREIGN JUDGMENTS (RECIPROCAL ENFORCEMENT) ACT 1933

(23 & 24 Geo 5 c 13)

An Act to make provision for the enforcement in the United Kingdom of judgments given in foreign countries which accord reciprocal treatment to judgments given in the United Kingdom, for facilitating the enforcement in foreign countries of judgments given in the United Kingdom, and for other purposes in connection with the matters aforesaid.   [13 April 1933]

Note. For procedure under this Act, see RSC Ord 71, r 13.

For modification of Part I of this Act, see Administration of Justice Act 1956, s 51 (p 2173).

PART I*

Registration of Foreign Judgments

1. Power to extend Part I of Act to foreign countries giving reciprocal treatment—(*1*) *His Majesty, if he is satisfied that, in the event of the benefits conferred by*

---

* Part I of the Act has been applied to the Dominions, etc, by Reciprocal Enforcement of Judgments (General Application to His Majesty's Dominions, etc) Order 1933 (SR & O 1933 No 1073); Pakistan (SI 1958 No 141); India (SI 1958 No 425); Norway (SI 1962 No 636); Austria (SI 1962 No 1339); Israel (SI 1971 No 1039); Guernsey (SI 1973 No 610); Isle of Man (SI 1973 No 611); Jersey (SI 1973 No 612); Italy (SI 1973 No 1894); Tonga (SI 1980 No 1523); Suriname (SI 1981 No 735); Canada (SI 1987 No 468, as amended by SI 1987 No 2211, SI 1988 No 1304, SI 1988 No 1853, SI 1989 No 987 and SI 1991 No 1724); Reciprocal Enforcement of Judgments (Australian) Order 1994 (SI 1994 No 1901).

this Part of this Act being extended to judgments given in the superior courts of any foreign country, substantial reciprocity of treatment will be assured as respects the enforcement in that foreign country of judgments given in the superior courts of the United Kingdom, may by Order in Council direct—

    (*a*) *that this Part of this Act shall extend to that foreign country; and*

    (*b*) *that such courts of that foreign country as are specified in the Order shall be deemed superior courts of that country for the purposes of this Part of this Act.*

   (*2*) *Any judgment of a superior court of a foreign country to which this Part of this Act extends, other than a judgment of such a court given on appeal from a court which is not a superior court, shall be a judgment to which this Part of this Act applies, if—*

    (*a*) *it is final and conclusive as between the parties thereto; and*

    (*b*) *there is payable thereunder a sum of money, not being a sum payable in respect of taxes or other charges of a like nature or in respect of a fine or other penalty; and*

    (*c*) *it is given after the coming into operation of the Order in Council directing that this Part of this Act shall extend to that foreign country.*

   [(1) If, in the case of any foreign country, Her Majesty is satisfied that, in the event of the benefits conferred by this Part of this Act being extended to, or to any particular class of, judgments given in the courts of that country or in any particular class of those courts, substantial reciprocity of treatment will be assured as regards the enforcement in that country of similar judgments given in similar courts of the United Kingdom, She may by Order in Council direct—

    (a) that this Part of this Act shall extend to that country;

    (b) that such courts of that country as are specified in the Order shall be recognised courts of that country for the purposes of this Part of this Act; and

    (c) that judgments of any such recognised court, or such judgments of any class so specified, shall, if within subsection (2) of this section, be judgments to which this Part of this Act applies.

   (2) Subject to subsection (2A) of this section, a judgment of a recognised court is within this subsection if it satisfies the following conditions, namely—

    (a) it is either final and conclusive as between the judgment debtor and the judgment creditor or requires the former to make an interim payment to the latter; and

    (b) there is payable under it a sum of money, not being a sum payable in respect of taxes or other charges of a like nature or in respect of a fine or other penalty; and

    (c) it is given after the coming into force of the Order in Council which made that court a recognised court.

   (2A) The following judgments of a recognised court are not within subsection (2) of this section—

    (a) a judgment given by that court on appeal from a court which is not a recognised court;

    (b) a judgment or other instrument which is regarded for the purposes of its enforcement as a judgment of that court but which was given or made in another country;

    (c) a judgment given by that court in proceedings founded on a judgment of a court in another country and having as their object the enforcement of that judgment.]

Note. Sub-ss (1), (2), (2A) in square brackets substituted for sub-ss (1), (2) in italics by Civil Jurisdiction and Judgments Act 1982, s 35(1), Sch 10, para 1(1), (2), as from 14 November 1986.

   (3) For the purposes of this section, a judgment shall be deemed to be final and conclusive notwithstanding that an appeal may be pending against it, or that it may still be subject to appeal, in the courts of the country of the original court.

   (4) His Majesty may by a subsequent Order in Council vary or revoke any Order previously made under this section.

[(5) Any Order in Council made under this section before its amendment by the Civil Jurisdiction and Judgments Act 1982 which deems any court of a foreign country to be a superior court of that country for the purposes of this Part of this Act shall (without prejudice to subsection (4) of this section) have effect from the time of that amendment as if it provided for that court to be a recognised court of that country for those purposes, and for any final and conclusive judgment of that court, if within subsection (2) of this section, to be a judgment to which this Part of this Act applies.]

Note. Sub-s (5) added by Civil Jurisdiction and Judgments Act 1982, s 35(1), Sch 10, para 1(3), as from 1 January 1987.

2. Application for, and effect of, registration of foreign judgment—(1) A person, being a judgment creditor under a judgment to which this Part of this Act applies, may apply to the High Court at any time within six years after the date of the judgment, or, where there have been proceedings by way of appeal against the judgment, after the date of the last judgment given in those proceedings, to have the judgment registered in the High Court, and on any such application the court shall, subject to proof of the prescribed matters and to the other provisions of this Act, order the judgment to be registered:

Provided that a judgment shall not be registered if at the date of the application—
(a) it has been wholly satisfied; or
(b) it could not be enforced by execution in the country of the original court.

(2) Subject to the provisions of this Act with respect to the setting aside of registration—
(a) a registered judgment shall, for the purposes of execution, be of the same force and effect; and
(b) proceedings may be taken on a registered judgment; and
(c) the sum for which a judgment is registered shall carry interest; and
(d) the registering court shall have the same control over the execution of a registered judgment;

as if the judgment had been a judgment originally given in the registering court and entered on the date of registration:

Provided that execution shall not issue on the judgment so long as, under this Part of this Act and the Rules of Court made thereunder, it is competent for any party to make an application to have the registration of the judgment set aside, or, where such an application is made, until after the application has been finally determined.

(3) Where the sum payable under a judgment which is to be registered is expressed in a currency other than the currency of the United Kingdom, the judgment shall be registered as if it were a judgment for such sum in the currency of the United Kingdom as, on the basis of the rate of exchange prevailing at the date of the judgment of the original court, is equivalent to the sum so payable.

Note. Sub-s (3) repealed by Administration of Justice Act 1977, ss 4, 32(4), Sch 5.

(4) If at the date of the application for registration the judgment of the original court has been partly satisfied, the judgment shall not be registered in respect of the whole sum payable under the judgment of the original court, but only in respect of the balance remaining payable at that date.

(5) If, on an application for the registration of a judgment, it appears to the registering court that the judgment is in respect of different matters and that some, but not all, of the provisions of the judgment are such that if those provisions had been contained in separate judgments those judgments could properly have been registered, the judgment may be registered in respect of the provisions aforesaid but not in respect of any other provisions contained therein.

(6) In addition to the sum of money payable under the judgment of the original court, including any interest which by the law of the country of the original court becomes due under the judgment up to the time of registration, the judgment shall

be registered for the reasonable costs of and incidental to registration, including the costs of obtaining a certified copy of the judgment from the original court.

3.—(1) The power to make rules of court under section *ninety-nine of the Supreme Court of Judicature (Consolidation) Act 1925* [84 of the Supreme Court Act 1981], shall, subject to the provisions of this section, include power to make rules for the following purposes—

Note. Reference to 1981 Act substituted for reference to 1925 Act by Supreme Court Act 1981, s 152(1), Sch 5. For s 84 of that Act, see p 2798.

(a) For making provision with respect to the giving of security for costs by persons applying for the registration of judgments;

(b) For prescribing the matters to be proved on an application for the registration of a judgment and for regulating the mode of proving those matters;

(c) For providing for the service on the judgment debtor of notice of the registration of a judgment;

(d) For making provision with respect to the fixing of the period within which an application may be made to have the registration of the judgment set aside and with respect to the extension of the period so fixed;

(e) For prescribing the method by which any question arising under this Act whether a foreign judgment can be enforced by execution in the country of the original court, or what interest is payable under a foreign judgment under the law of the original court, is to be determined;

(f) For prescribing any matter which under this Part of this Act is to be prescribed.

(2) Rules made for the purposes of this Part of this Act shall be expressed to have, and shall have, effect subject to any such provisions contained in Orders in Council made under section one of this Act as are declared by the said Orders to be necessary for giving effect to the agreements made between His Majesty and foreign countries in relation to matters with respect to which there is power to make rules of court for the purposes of this Part of this Act.

4. Cases in which registered judgments must, or may, be set aside—(1) On an application in that behalf duly made by any party against whom a registered judgment may be enforced, the registration of the judgment—

(a) shall be set aside if the registering court is satisfied—

(i) that the judgment is not a judgment to which this Part of this Act applies or was registered in contravention of the foregoing provisions of this Act; or

(ii) that the courts of the country of the original court had no jurisdiction in the circumstances of the case; or

(iii) that the judgment debtor, being the defendant in the proceedings in the original court, did not (notwithstanding that process may have been duly served on him in accordance with the law of the country of the original court) receive notice of those proceedings in sufficient time to enable him to defend the proceedings and did not appear; or

(iv) that the judgment was obtained by fraud; or

(v) that the enforcement of the judgment would be contrary to public policy in the country of the registering court; or

(vi) that the rights under the judgment are not vested in the person by whom the application for registration was made;

(b) may be set aside if the registering court is satisfied that the matter in dispute in the proceedings in the original court had previously to the date of the judgment in the original court been the subject of a final and conclusive judgment by a court having jurisdiction in the matter.

(2) For the purposes of this section the courts of the country of the original court shall, subject to the provisions of subsection (3) of this section, be deemed to have had jurisdiction—

(a) in the case of a judgment given in an action in personam—
    (i) if the judgment debtor, being a defendant in the original court, submitted to the jurisdiction of that court by voluntarily appearing in the proceedings *otherwise than for the purpose of protecting, or obtaining the release of, property seized, or threatened with seizure, in the proceedings or of contesting the jurisdiction of that court*; or
    (ii) if the judgment debtor was plaintiff in, or counterclaimed in, the proceedings in the original court; or
    (iii) if the judgment debtor, being a defendant in the original court, had before the commencement of the proceedings agreed, in respect of the subject matter of the proceedings, to submit to the jurisdiction of that court or of the courts of the country of that court; or
    (iv) if the judgment debtor, being a defendant in the original court, was at the time when the proceedings were instituted resident in, or being a body corporate had its principal place of business in, the country of that court; or
    (v) if the judgment debtor, being a defendant in the original court, had an office or place of business in the country of that court and the proceedings in that court were in respect of a transaction effected through or at that office or place;
(b) in the case of a judgment given in an action of which the subject matter was immovable property or in an action in rem of which the subject matter was movable property, if the property in question was at the time of the proceedings in the original court situate in the country of that court;
(c) in the case of a judgment given in an action other than any such action as is mentioned in paragraph (a) or paragraph (b) of this subsection, if the jurisdiction of the original court is recognised by the law of the registering court.

(3) Notwithstanding anything in subsection (2) of this section, the courts of the country of the original court shall not be deemed to have had jurisdiction—
(a) if the subject matter of the proceedings was immovable property outside the country of the original court; or
(b) *except in the cases mentioned in sub-paragraphs (i), (ii) and (iii) of paragraph (a) and in paragraph (c) of subsection (2) of this section, if the bringing of the proceedings in the original court was contrary to an agreement under which the dispute in question was to be settled otherwise than by proceedings in the courts of the country of that court;* or
(c) if the judgment debtor, being a defendant in the original proceedings, was a person who under the rules of public international law was entitled to immunity from the jurisdiction of the courts of the country of the original court and did not submit to the jurisdiction of that court.

Note. Words in italics in sub-s (2)(a)(i), and sub-s (3)(b), repealed by Civil Jurisdiction and Judgments Act 1982, s 54, Sch 14, as from 24 August 1982 except in relation to judgments registered under Part I of that Act before that date: s 53(2), Sch 13, Part II, paras 8(2), 9(2).

5. Powers of registering court on application to set aside registration—(1) If, on an application to set aside the registration of a judgment, the applicant satisfies the registering court either that an appeal is pending, or that he is entitled and intends to appeal, against the judgment, the court, if it thinks fit, may, on such terms as it may think just, either set aside the registration or adjourn the application to set aside the registration until after the expiration of such period as appears to the court to be reasonably sufficient to enable the applicant to take the necessary steps to have the appeal disposed of by the competent tribunal.

(2) Where the registration of a judgment is set aside under the last foregoing subsection, or solely for the reason that the judgment was not at the date of the application for registration enforceable by execution in the country of the original court, the setting aside of the registration shall not prejudice a further application

to register the judgment when the appeal has been disposed of or if and when the judgment becomes enforceable by execution in that country, as the case may be.

(3) Where the registration of a judgment is set aside solely for the reason that the judgment, notwithstanding that it had at the date of the application for registration been partly satisfied, was registered for the whole sum payable thereunder, the registering court shall, on the application of the judgment creditor, order judgment to be registered for the balance remaining payable at that date.

6. Foreign judgments which can be registered not to be enforceable otherwise. No proceedings for the recovery of a sum payable under a foreign judgment, being a judgment to which this Part of this Act applies, other than proceedings by way of registration of the judgment, shall be entertained by any court in the United Kingdom.

7. Power to apply Part I of Act to British dominions, protectorates and mandated territories—(1) His Majesty may by Order in Council direct that this Part of this Act shall apply to His Majesty's dominions outside the United Kingdom and to judgments obtained in the courts of the said dominions as it applies to foreign countries and judgments obtained in the courts of foreign countries, and, in the event of His Majesty so directing, this Act shall have effect accordingly and Part II of the Administration of Justice Act 1920 shall cease to have effect except in relation to those parts of the said dominions to which it extends at the date of the Order.

Note. See also Reciprocal Enforcement of Judgments (General Application to His Majesty's Dominions, etc) Order 1933 (SR & O 1933 No 1073), amended by Zimbabwe (Independence and Membership of Commonwealth) (Consequential Provisions) Order 1980, SI 1980 No 701, art 7, Schedule, para 4(1).

For Administration of Justice Act 1920, Part. II, see p 2045.

(2) If at any time after His Majesty has directed as aforesaid an Order in Council is made under section one of this Act extending Part I of this Act to any part of His Majesty's dominions to which the said Part II extends as aforesaid, the said Part II shall cease to have effect in relation to that part of His Majesty's dominions.

Note. For Administration of Justice Act 1920, Part II, see p 2045.

(3) References in this section to His Majesty's dominions outside the United Kingdom shall be construed as including references to any territories which are under His Majesty's protection and to any territories in respect of which a mandate under the League of Nations has been accepted by His Majesty.

PART II

Miscellaneous and General

8. General effect of certain foreign judgments—(1) Subject to the provisions of this section, a judgment to which Part I of this Act applies or would have applied if a sum of money had been payable thereunder, whether it can be registered or not, and whether, if it can be registered, it is registered or not, shall be recognised in any court in the United Kingdom as conclusive between the parties thereto in all proceedings founded on the same cause of action and may be relied on by way of defence or counterclaim in any such proceedings.

(2) This section shall not apply in the case of any judgment—
(a) where the judgment has been registered and the registration thereof has been set aside on some ground other than—
   (i) that a sum of money was not payable under the judgment; or
   (ii) that the judgment had been wholly or partly satisfied; or
   (iii) that at the date of the application the judgment could not be enforced by execution in the country of the original court; or

(b) where the judgment has not been registered, it is shown (whether it could have been registered or not) that if it had been registered the registration thereof would have been set aside on an application for that purpose on some ground other than one of the grounds specified in paragraph (a) of this subsection.

(3) Nothing in this section shall be taken to prevent any court in the United Kingdom recognising any judgment as conclusive of any matter of law or fact decided therein if that judgment would have been so recognised before the passing of this Act.

9. Power to make foreign judgments unenforceable in United Kingdom if no reciprocity—(1) If it appears to His Majesty that the treatment in respect of recognition and enforcement accorded by the courts of any foreign country to judgments given in the *superior* courts of the United Kingdom is substantially less favourable than that accorded by the courts of the United Kingdom to judgments of the *superior* courts of that country, His Majesty may by Order in Council apply this section to that country.

Note. 'Superior' repealed in both places where it occurs by Civil Jurisdiction and Judgments Act 1982, ss 35(1), 54, Sch 10, para 2, Sch 14, as from 14 November 1986.

(2) Except in so far as His Majesty may by Order in Council under this section otherwise direct, no proceedings shall be entertained in any court in the United Kingdom for the recovery of any sum alleged to be payable under a judgment given in a court of a country to which this section applies.

(3) His Majesty may by a subsequent Order in Council vary or revoke any Order previously made under this section.

10. Issue of certificates of judgments obtained in the United Kingdom. *Where a judgment under which a sum of money is payable, not being a sum payable in respect of taxes or other charges of a like nature or in respect of a fine or other penalty, has been entered in the High Court against any person and the judgment creditor is desirous of enforcing the judgment in a foreign country to which Part I of this Act applies, the court shall, on an application made by the judgment creditor and on payment of such fee as may be fixed for the purposes of this section under section two hundred and thirteen of the Supreme Court of Judicature (Consolidation) Act 1925 [130 of the Supreme Court Act 1981] issue to the judgment creditor a certified copy of the judgment, together with a certificate containing such particulars with respect to the action, including the causes of action, and the rate of interest, if any, payable on the sum payable under the judgment, as may be prescribed:*

Provided that, where execution of a judgment is stayed for any period pending an appeal or for any other reason, an application shall not be made under this section with respect to the judgment until the expiration of that period.

Note. Reference to Supreme Court Act 1981 substituted for reference to Act of 1925 by Supreme Court Act 1981, s 152(1), Sch 5.

[10. Provision for issue of copies of, and certificates in connection with, UK judgments—(1) Rules may make provision for enabling any judgment creditor wishing to secure the enforcement in a foreign country to which Part I of this Act extends of a judgment to which this subsection applies, to obtain, subject to any conditions specified in the rules—

(a) a copy of the judgment; and
(b) a certificate giving particulars relating to the judgment and the proceedings in which it was given.

(2) Subsection (1) applies to any judgment given by a court or tribunal in the United Kingdom under which a sum of money is payable, not being a sum payable in respect of taxes or other charges of a like nature or in respect of a fine or other penalty.

(3) In this section 'rules'—

(a) in relation to judgments given by a court, means rules of court;

(b) in relation to judgments given by any other tribunal, means rules or regulations made by the authority having power to make rules or regulations regulating the procedure of that tribunal.]

[10A. Arbitration awards. The provisions of this Act, except sections 1(5) and 6, shall apply, as they apply to a judgment, in relation to an award in proceedings on an arbitration which has, in pursuance of the law in force in the place where it was made, become enforceable in the same manner as a judgment given by a court in that place.]

Note. Section 10 substituted and s 10A inserted (both in square brackets) by Civil Jurisdiction and Judgments Act 1982, s 35(1), Sch 10, paras 3, 4, as from 14 November 1986.

11. Interpretation—(1) In this Act, unless the context otherwise requires, the following expressions have the meanings hereby assigned to them respectively, that is to say—

'Appeal' includes any proceedings by way of discharging or setting aside a judgment or an application for a new trial or a stay of execution;

'Country of the original court' means the country in which the original court is situated;

['Court', except in section 10 of this Act, includes a tribunal;]

'Judgment' means a judgment or order given or made by a court in any civil proceedings, or a judgment or order given or made by a court in any criminal proceedings for the payment of a sum of money in respect of compensation or damages to an injured party;

'Judgment creditor' means the person in whose favour the judgment was given and includes any person in whom the rights under the judgment have become vested by succession or assignment or otherwise;

'Judgment debtor' means the person against whom the judgment was given, and includes any person against whom the judgment is enforceable under the law of the original court;

'Judgments given in the superior courts of the United Kingdom' means judgments given in the High Court in England, the Court of Session in Scotland, the High Court in Northern Ireland, the Court of Chancery of the County Palatine of Lancaster or the Court of Chancery of the County Palatine of Durham, and includes judgments given in any courts on appeals against any judgments so given;

'Original court' in relation to any judgment means the court by which the judgment was given;

'Prescribed' means prescribed by rules of court;

'Registration' means registration under Part I of this Act, and the expressions 'register' and 'registered' shall be construed accordingly;

'Registered court' in relation to any judgment means the court to which an application to register the judgment is made.

Note. Words 'the Court of Chancery ... County Palatine of Durham' in definition 'Judgments given in the superior courts of the United Kingdom' repealed by Courts Act 1971, s 56(4), Sch 11, Part II.

Definition 'Court' inserted and definition 'Judgments given in the superior courts of the United Kingdom' repealed by Civil Jurisdiction and Judgments Act 1982, ss 35(1), 54, Sch 10, para 5, Sch 14, as from 14 November 1986.

(2) For the purposes of this Act, the expression 'action in personam' shall not be deemed to include any matrimonial cause or any proceedings in connection with any of the following matters, that is to say, matrimonial matters, administration of the estates of deceased persons, bankruptcy, winding up of companies, lunacy, or guardianship of infants.

12. Application to Scotland. This Act in its application to Scotland shall have effect subject to the following modifications—

(a) For any reference to the High Court (*except in section eleven of this Act*) there shall be substituted a reference to the Court of Session:

(b) The Court of Session shall, subject to the provisions of subsection (2) of section three of this Act, have power by Act of Sederunt to make rules for the purposes specified in subsection (1) of the said section:

(c) Registration under Part I of this Act shall be effected by registering in the Books of Council and Session or in such manner as the Court of Session may by Act of Sederunt prescribe:

(d) *For any reference to section two hundred and thirteen of the Supreme Court of Judicature (Consolidation) Act 1925, there shall be substituted a reference to the Courts of Law Fees (Scotland) Act 1895:*

(e) For any reference to the entering of a judgment there shall be substituted a reference to the signing of the interlocutor embodying the judgment.

Note. Words in italics in para (a) and whole of para (d) repealed by Civil Jurisdiction and Judgments Act 1982, s 54, Sch 14, as from 1 January 1987.

13. Application to Northern Ireland. This Act in its application to Northern Ireland shall have effect subject to the following modifications—

(a) References to the High Court shall, unless the context otherwise requires, be construed as references to the High Court in Northern Ireland:

(b) For the references to section ninety-nine *and section two hundred and thirteen* of the Supreme Court of Judicature (Consolidation) Act 1925, there shall be substituted [*respectively*, reference to sections 55 *and 116* of the Judicature (Northern Ireland) Act 1978].

Note. Words in square brackets substituted by Judicature (Northern Ireland) Act 1978, s 122(1), Sch 5. Words in italics repealed by Civil Jurisdiction and Judgments Act 1982, s 54, Sch 14, as from 1 January 1987.

14. Short title. This Act may be cited as the Foreign Judgments (Reciprocal Enforcement) Act 1933.

ADMINISTRATION OF JUSTICE (MISCELLANEOUS PROVISIONS) ACT 1933

(23 & 24 Geo 5 c 36)

* * * * *

7. Costs in Crown proceedings—(1) In any civil proceedings to which the Crown is a party in any court having power to award costs in cases between subjects, and in any arbitration to which the Crown is a party, the costs of and incidental to the proceedings shall be in the discretion of the court or arbitrator to be exercised in the same manner and on the same principles as in cases between subjects, and the court or arbitrator shall have power to make an order for the payment of costs by or to the Crown accordingly:

Provided that—

(a) in the case of proceedings to which by reason of any enactment or otherwise the Attorney-General, a Government department or any officer of the Crown as such is required to be made a party, the court or arbitrator shall have regard to the nature of the proceedings and the character and circumstances in which the Attorney-General, the department or officer of the Crown appears, and may in the exercise of its or his discretion order any other party to the proceedings to pay the costs of the Attorney-General, department or officer, whatever may be the result of the proceedings: and

(b) nothing in this section shall affect the power of the court or arbitrator to order, or any enactment providing for, the payment of costs out of any particular fund or property, or any enactment expressly relieving any department or officer of the Crown of the liability to pay costs.

(2) In this section the expression 'civil proceedings' includes *proceedings by petition of right and* proceedings by the Crown in the High Court or a county court for the recovery of fines or penalties, and references to proceedings to which the Crown is a party include references to proceedings to which the Attorney-General or any Government department or any officer of the Crown as such is a party, so, however, that the Crown shall not be deemed to be a party to any proceedings by reason only that the proceedings are proceedings by the Attorney-General on the relation of some other person.

(3) *This section shall apply to proceedings pending at the commencement of this Act.*

*　　*　　*　　*　　*

Note. Proceedings by petition of right were abolished by Crown Proceedings Act 1947, s 23, Sch 1, and Petitions of Right Act 1860 was repealed by s 39 of, and Sch 2 to, that Act. Sub-s (3) repealed by Statute Law (Repeals) Act 1993, s 1(1), Sch 1, Part I, as from 5 November 1993.

ADMINISTRATION OF JUSTICE (APPEALS) ACT 1934

(24 & 25 Geo 5 c 40)

An Act to provide that no appeal shall lie from the Court of Appeal to the House of Lords except with the leave of that Court or the House of Lords, to make further provision as respects appeals from county courts, and for purposes connected with the matters aforesaid.   [25 July 1934]

1. Restriction on appeals from Court of Appeal to House of Lords—(1) No appeal shall lie to the House of Lords from any order or judgment made or given by the Court of Appeal after the first day of October nineteen hundred and thirty-four, except with the leave of that Court or of the House of Lords.

(2) The House of Lords may by order provide for the hearing and determination by a Committee of that House of petitions for leave to appeal from the Court of Appeal:

Provided that section five of the Appellate Jurisdiction Act 1876, shall apply to the hearing and determination of any such petition by a Committee of the House as it applies to the hearing and determination of an appeal by the House.

(3) Nothing in this section shall affect any restriction existing, apart from this section, on the bringing of appeals from the Court of Appeal to the House of Lords.

*　　*　　*　　*　　*

3. Short title and extent—(1) This Act may be cited as the Administration of Justice (Appeals) Act 1934.

(2) This Act shall not extend to Scotland or Northern Ireland.

SUPREME COURT OF JUDICATURE (AMENDMENT) ACT 1935

(25 Geo 5 c 2)

*　　*　　*　　*　　*

4. Certain evidence in nullity proceedings to be in camera. *The principal Act shall have effect as if the following section were inserted after section one hundred and ninety-eight thereof—*

'**198A.** *In any proceedings for nullity of marriage, evidence on the question of sexual capacity shall be heard in camera unless in any case the judge is satisfied that in the interests of justice any such evidence ought to be heard in open court.*'

Note. Repealed by Matrimonial Causes Act 1950, s 34, Schedule, and replaced by ibid, s 32(4) (p 2154). See now Matrimonial Causes Act 1973, s 48(2) (p 2522), replacing Matrimonial Causes Act 1965, s 43(3) (p 2248).

*　　*　　*　　*　　*

LAW REFORM (MARRIED WOMEN AND TORTFEASORS) ACT 1935

(25 & 26 Geo 5 c 30)

* * * * *

2. Property of married women—(1) Subject to the provisions of this Part of this Act all property which—

(a) immediately before the passing of this Act was the separate property of a married woman or held for her separate use in equity; or

(b) belongs at the time of her marriage to a woman married after the passing of this Act; or

(c) after the passing of this Act is acquired by or devolves upon a married woman,

shall belong to her in all respects as if she were a feme sole and may be disposed of accordingly:

Provided that nothing in this subsection shall interfere with or render inoperative any restriction upon anticipation or alienation attached to the enjoyment of any property by virtue of any provision attaching such a restriction, contained in any Act passed before the passing of this Act, or in any instrument executed before the first day of January, nineteen hundred and thirty-six.

(2) Any instrument executed on or after the first day of January, nineteen hundred and thirty-six, shall, in so far as it purports to attach to the enjoyment of any property by a woman any restriction upon anticipation or alienation which could not have been attached to the enjoyment of that property by a man, be void.

(3) For the purposes of the provisions of this section relating to restrictions upon anticipation or alienation—

(a) *an instrument attaching such a restriction as aforesaid executed on or after the first day of January, nineteen hundred and thirty-six, in pursuance of an obligation imposed before that date to attach such a restriction shall be deemed to have been executed before the said first day of January;*

(b) *a provision contained in an instrument made in exercise of a special power of appointment shall be deemed to be contained in that instrument only and not in the instrument by which the power was created; and*

(c) *the will of any testator who dies after the thirty-first day of December, nineteen hundred and forty-five, shall (notwithstanding the actual date of the execution thereof) be deemed to have been executed after the first day of January, nineteen hundred and thirty-six.*

Note. Word in italics repealed by Married Women (Restraint Upon Anticipation) Act 1949, s 1, Sch 2.

* * * *

4. Savings—(1) Nothing in this Part of this Act shall—

(a) during coverture which began before the first day of January, eighteen hundred and eighty-three, affect any property to which the title (whether vested or contingent, and whether in possession, reversion, or remainder) of a married woman accrued before that date, except property held for her separate use in equity;

(b) affect any legal proceeding in respect of any tort if proceedings had been instituted in respect thereof before the passing of this Act;

(c) enable any judgment or order against a married woman in respect of a contract entered into, or debt or obligation incurred, before the passing of this Act, to be enforced in bankruptcy or to be enforced otherwise than against her property.

(2) For the avoidance of doubt it is hereby declared that nothing in this Part of this Act—

(a) renders the husband of a married woman liable in respect of any contract entered into, or debt or obligation incurred, by her after the marriage in respect of which he would not have been liable if this Act had not been passed;

(b) exempts the husband of a married woman from liability in respect of any contract entered into, or debt or obligation (not being a debt or obligation arising out of the commission of a tort) incurred, by her after the marriage in respect of which he would have been liable if this Act had not been passed;

(c) prevents a husband and wife from acquiring, holding, and disposing of, any property jointly or as tenants in common, or from rendering themselves, or being rendered, jointly liable in respect of any tort, contract, debt or obligation, and of suing and being sued either in tort or in contract or otherwise, in like manner as if they were not married;

(d) prevents the exercise of any joint power given to a husband and wife.

*   *   *   *   *

MATRIMONIAL CAUSES ACT 1937*

(1 Edw 8 & 1 Geo 6 c 57)

An Act to amend the law relating to marriage and divorce.   [*30 July 1937*]

* The whole Act, except s 11, repealed by Matrimonial Causes Act 1950, s 34(1), Schedule.

1. Restriction on petitions for divorce during first three years after marriage—

(*1*) *No petition for divorce shall be presented to the High Court unless at the date of the presentation of the petition three years have passed since the date of the marriage:*

Provided that a judge of the High Court may, upon application being made to him in accordance with rules of court, allow a petition to be presented before three years have passed on the ground that the case is one of exceptional hardship suffered by the petitioner or of exceptional depravity on the part of the respondent, but if it appears to the court at the hearing of the petition, that the petitioner obtained leave to present the petition by any misrepresentation or concealment of the nature of the case, the court may, if it pronounces a decree nisi, do so subject to the condition that no application to make the decree absolute shall be made until after the expiration of three years from the date of the marriage, or may dismiss the petition, without prejudice to any petition which may be brought after the expiration of the said three years upon the same, or substantially the same, facts as those proved in support of the petition so dismissed.

(*2*) *In determining any application under this section for leave to present a petition before the expiration of three years from the date of the marriage, the judge shall have regard to the interests of any children of the marriage and to the question whether there is reasonable probability of a reconciliation between the parties before the expiration of the said three years.*

(*3*) *Nothing in this section shall be deemed to prohibit the presentation of a petition based upon matters which have occurred before the expiration of three years from the date of the marriage.*

Note. See now Matrimonial Causes Act 1973, s 3 (p 2472), replacing Matrimonial Causes Act 1965, ss 2, 5(5) (pp 2224, 2226), replacing Matrimonial Causes Act 1950, s 2(1), (2), (3) (p 2135).

This section did not apply to petitions brought under Matrimonial Causes (War Marriages) Act 1944. See Matrimonial Causes Act 1950, s 2(4) (p 2135), repealed by Matrimonial Causes Act 1965.

2. Grounds of petition for divorce. *The following section shall be substituted for section one hundred and seventy-six of the Supreme Court of Judicature (Consolidation) Act 1925 (hereinafter called 'the principal Act')—*

'**176A**. *A petition for divorce may be presented to the High Court (in this part of this Act referred to as 'the Court') either by the husband or the wife on the ground that the respondent—*

(a) *has since the celebration of the marriage committed adultery; or*

(b) *has deserted the petitioner without cause for a period of at least three years immediately preceding the presentation of the petition; or*

(c) *has since the celebration of the marriage treated the petitioner with cruelty; or* (*d*) *is incurably of unsound mind and has been continuously under care and treatment for a period of at least five years immediately preceding the presentation of the petition, and by the wife on the ground that her husband has, since the celebration of the marriage, been guilty of rape, sodomy or bestiality.*'

Note. See now Matrimonial Causes Act 1973, s 1(1), (2) (p 2471), replacing Divorce Reform Act 1969, ss 1, 2(1) (p 2319), replacing Matrimonial Causes Act 1965, s 1(1) (p 2223), replacing Matrimonial Causes Act 1950, s 1(1) (p 2120).

3. Definition of 'care and treatment' in relation to insanity. *For the purposes of section one hundred and seventy-six of the principal Act, as amended by this Act, a person of unsound mind shall be deemed to be under care and treatment—*

Note. For Supreme Court of Judicature (Consolidation) Act 1925, s 176 (repealed), see p 2054.

    (*a*) *while he is detained in pursuance of any order or inquisition under the Lunacy and Mental Treatment Acts 1890 to 1930, or of any order or warrant under the Army Act, the Air Force Act, the Naval Discipline Act, the Naval Enlistment Act 1884 or the Yarmouth Naval Hospital Act 1931, or is being detained as a criminal lunatic or in pursuance of an order made under the Criminal Lunatics Act 1884;*

    (*b*) *while he is receiving treatment as a voluntary patient under the Mental Treatment Act 1930, being treatment which follows without any interval a period of such detention as aforesaid;*

and not otherwise.

Note. Extended by Law Reform (Miscellaneous Provisions) Act 1949, s 3 (repealed).
    Repealed and re-enacted by Matrimonial Causes Act 1950, s 1(2) (p 2120), replaced by Matrimonial Causes Act 1965, s 1(3) (p 2223), repealed by Divorce Reform Act 1969, s 9(2) Sch 2 and not replaced.

4. Duty of Court on presentation of petition for divorce. *The following section shall be substituted for section one hundred and seventy-eight of the principal Act—*

    '**178**—(*1*) *On a petition for divorce it shall be the duty of the court to inquire, so far as it reasonably can into the facts alleged and whether there has been any connivance or condonation on the part of the petitioner and whether any collusion exists between the parties and also to inquire into any countercharge which is made against the petitioner.*

    (*2*) *If the court is satisfied on the evidence that—*

    (*i*) *the case for the petition has been proved; and*

    (*ii*) *where the ground of the petition is adultery, the petitioner has not in any manner been accessory to, or connived at, or condoned the adultery, or where the ground of the petition is cruelty the petitioner has not in any manner condoned the cruelty; and*

    (*iii*) *the petition is not presented or prosecuted in collusion with the respondent or either of the respondents,*

the court shall pronounce a decree of divorce, but if the court is not satisfied with respect to any of the aforesaid matters, it shall dismiss the petition:

    Provided that the court shall not be bound to pronounce a decree of divorce and may dismiss the petition if it finds that the petitioner has during the marriage been guilty of adultery or if, in the opinion of the court, the petitioner has been guilty—

    (*a*) *of unreasonable delay in presenting or prosecuting the petition; or*

    (*b*) *of cruelty towards the other party to the marriage; or*

    (*c*) *where the ground of the petition is adultery or cruelty, of having without reasonable excuse deserted, or having without reasonable excuse wilfully separated himself or herself from, the other party before the adultery or cruelty complained of; or*

    (*d*) *where the ground of the petition is adultery or unsoundness of mind or desertion, of such wilful neglect or misconduct as has conduced to the adultery or unsoundness of mind or desertion.*'

Note. Substituted s 178 repealed by Matrimonial Causes Act 1950, s 34(1), Schedule. See now Matrimonial Causes Act 1973, ss 1(3), (4), 2(1), (2) (p 2471), replacing Divorce Reform Act 1969, ss 2(2), (3), 3(3) (pp 2319, 2320), replacing Matrimonial Causes Act 1965, s 5(1), (3), (4) (p 2225), replacing Matrimonial Causes Act 1950, s 4 (p 2122), as amended by Matrimonial Causes Act 1963, s 4.

5. Decree of judicial separation. *The following subsections shall be substituted for subsections (1) and (2) of section one hundred and eighty-five of the principal Act:*

'(1)　*A petition for judicial separation may be presented to the court either by the husband or the wife on any grounds on which a petition for divorce might have been presented, or on the ground of failure to comply with a decree for restitution of conjugal rights or on any ground on which a decree for divorce a mensa et thoro might have been pronounced immediately before the commencement of the Matrimonial Causes Act 1857, and the foregoing provisions of this Part of the Act relating to the duty of the court on the presentation of a petition for divorce, and the circumstances in which such a petition shall or may be granted or dismissed, shall apply in like manner to a petition for judicial separation.*

(2)　*Where the court in accordance with the said provisions grants a decree of judicial separation, it shall no longer be obligatory for the petitioner to cohabit with the respondent.'*

Note. Repealed by Matrimonial Causes Act 1950, s 34(1), Schedule. See now Matrimonial Causes Act 1973, ss 17, 18 (pp 2479, 2480), replacing Matrimonial Causes Act 1965, s 12 (p 2229), replacing Matrimonial Causes Act 1950, s 14(1), (2) (p 2125).

6. Divorce proceedings after grant of judicial separation or other relief—(1) *A person shall not be prevented from presenting a petition for divorce, or the court from pronouncing a decree of divorce, by reason only that the petitioner has at any time been granted a judicial separation or an order under the Summary Jurisdiction (Separation and Maintenance) Acts 1895 to 1925, upon the same or substantially the same facts as those proved in support of the petition for divorce.*

Note. Summary Jurisdiction (Separation and Maintenance) Acts 1895 to 1925 are Summary Jurisdiction (Married Women) Act 1895, Licensing Act 1902, s 5, Married Women (Maintenance) Act 1920, and Summary Jurisdiction (Separation and Maintenance) Act 1925.

(2)　*On any such petition for divorce, the court may treat the decree of judicial separation or the said order as sufficient proof of the adultery, desertion, or other ground on which it was granted, but the court shall not pronounce a decree of divorce without receiving evidence from the petitioner.*

(3)　*For the purposes of any petition for divorce, a period of desertion immediately preceding the institution of proceedings for a decree of judicial separation or an order under the said Acts having the effect of such a decree shall, if the parties have not resumed cohabitation and the decree or order has been continuously in force since the granting thereof, be deemed immediately to precede the presentation of the petition for divorce.*

Note. See now Matrimonial Causes Act 1973, s 4 (p 2473), replacing Matrimonial Causes Act 1965, s 3 (p 2224), replacing Matrimonial Causes Act 1950, s 7 (p 2123).

7. New grounds for decree of nullity—(1) *In addition to any other grounds on which a marriage is by law void or voidable, a marriage shall be voidable on the ground—*

(a)　*that the marriage has not been consummated owing to the wilful refusal of the respondent to consummate the marriage; or*

(b)　*that either party to the marriage was at the time of the marriage of unsound mind or a mental defective within the meaning of the Mental Deficiency Acts 1913 to 1927, or subject to recurrent fits of insanity or epilepsy; or*

(c)　*that the respondent was at the time of the marriage suffering from venereal disease in a communicable form; or*

(d)　*that the respondent was at the time of the marriage pregnant by some other person other than the petitioner:*

Provided that, in the cases specified in paragraphs (b), (c) and (d) of this subsection, the court shall not grant a decree unless it is satisfied—

(i)　*that the petitioner was at the time of the marriage ignorant of the facts alleged;*

(ii)　*that proceedings were instituted within a year from the date of the marriage; and*

(iii)　*that marital intercourse with the consent of the petitioner has not taken place since the discovery by the petitioner of the existence of the grounds for a decree.*

Note. Subsection (1) replaced by Matrimonial Causes Act 1950, s 8(1) (p 2123), replaced by Matrimonial Causes Act 1965, s 9(1), (2) (p 2228) which was repealed by Nullity of Marriage Act 1971, s 7(3), except in relation to marriages taking place before 1 August 1971.

(*2*) *Any child born of a marriage avoided pursuant to paragraphs* (*b*) *or* (*c*) *of the last foregoing subsection shall be a legitimate child of the parties thereto notwithstanding that the marriage is so avoided.*

Note. Subsection (2) repealed by Law Reform (Miscellaneous Provisions) Act 1949, s 4(2). See now Matrimonial Causes Act 1973, Sch 1, para 12 (p 2527), replacing Matrimonial Causes Act 1965, s 11 (p 2229), replacing Matrimonial Causes Act 1950, s 9 (p 2123).

(*3*) *Nothing in this section shall be construed as validating any marriage which is by law void, but with respect to which a decree of nullity has not been granted.*

Note. Subsection (3) repealed by Matrimonial Causes Act 1950, s 8(2), replaced by Matrimonial Causes Act 1965, s 9(3) (p 2228), which was repealed by Nullity of Marriage Act 1971, s 7(3), except in relation to marriages taking place before 1 August 1971.

For the grounds on which a marriage celebrated after 31 July 1971 is void or voidable, see Matrimonial Causes Act 1973, ss 11, 12 (pp 2476, 2477), replacing Nullity of Marriage Act 1971, ss 1, 2 (pp 2396, 2397).

8. Proceedings for decree of presumption of death and dissolution of marriage—(*1*) *Any married person who alleges that reasonable grounds exist for supposing that the other party to the marriage is dead may present a petition to the court to have it presumed that the other party is dead and to have the marriage dissolved, and the court if satisfied that such reasonable grounds exist, may make a decree of presumption of death and of dissolution of the marriage.*

(*2*) *In any such proceedings the fact that for a period of seven years or upwards the other party to the marriage has been continually absent from the petitioner, and the petitioner has no reason to believe that the other party has been living within that time, shall be evidence that he or she is dead until the contrary is proved.*

(*3*) *Sections one hundred and eighty-one to one hundred and eighty-four inclusive of the principal Act shall apply to a petition and a decree under this section as they apply to a petition for divorce and a decree of divorce respectively.*

Note. See now Matrimonial Causes Act 1973, s 19 (p 2480), replacing Matrimonial Causes Act 1965, s 14 (p 2230), replacing Matrimonial Causes Act 1950, s 16 (p 2126).

For Supreme Court of Judicature (Consolidation) Act 1925, ss 181–184 (repealed), see pp 2056–2057.

9. Presentation of delay in application for decree absolute. *Section one hundred and eighty-three of the principal Act shall be amended by adding thereto a subsection as follows—*

'(*3*) *Where a decree nisi has been obtained, whether before or after the passing of this Act, and no application for the decree to be made absolute has been made by the party who obtained the decree, then at any time after the expiration of three months from the earliest date on which that party could have made such an application, the party against whom the decree nisi has been granted shall be at liberty to apply to the court and the court shall, on such application, have power to make the decree absolute, reverse the decree nisi, require further inquiry or otherwise deal with the case as the court thinks fit.*'

Note. Repealed by Matrimonial Causes Act 1950, s 34(1), Schedule. See now Matrimonial Causes Act 1973, ss 9(2), 15 (pp 2475, 2478), replacing Matrimonial Causes Act 1965, ss 7(2), 10 (pp 2227, 2229), replacing Matrimonial Causes Act 1950, s 12(3) (p 2124).

10. Amendments as to maintenance, settlement of property, &c.—(*1*) *When a petition for divorce or nullity of marriage has been presented, proceedings under section one hundred and ninety, section one hundred and ninety-one, section one hundred and ninety-two or subsection (3) of section one hundred and ninety-three of the principal Act (which, respectively, confer power on the court to order the provision of alimony, the settlement of the wife's property, the application of property which is the subject of marriage settlements, and the securing of money for the benefit of the children) may, subject to and in accordance with rules of court, be commenced at any time after the presentation of the petition:*

Note. For Supreme Court of Judicature (Consolidation) Act 1925, ss 190–192, 193(3) (repealed), see pp 2060–2062.

Provided that no order under any of the said sections or under the said subsection (other than an interim order for the payment of alimony under section one hundred and ninety) shall be made unless and until a decree nisi has been pronounced, and no such order, save in so far as it relates to the preparation, execution, or approval of a deed or instrument and no settlement made in pursuance of any such order, shall take effect unless and until the decree is made absolute.

Note. See now Matrimonial Causes Act 1973, ss 23, 24 (pp 2484, 2487), replacing Matrimonial Proceedings and Property Act 1970, ss 2, 4, 24 (pp 2345, 2346, 2358), replacing Matrimonial Causes Act 1965, ss 18, 19 (p 2232).

(2)   The said section one hundred and ninety shall apply in any case where a petition for divorce or judicial separation is presented by the wife on the ground of her husband's insanity as if for the references to the husband there were substituted references to the wife, and for the references to the wife there were substituted references to the husband, and in any such case and in any case where a petition for divorce, nullity, or judicial separation, is presented by the husband on the ground of his wife's insanity or mental deficiency, the court may order the payments of alimony or maintenance under the said section to be made to such persons having charge of the respondent as the court may direct.

Note. See now Matrimonial Causes Act 1973, ss 22, 23, 40 (pp 2482, 2484, 2515), replacing Matrimonial Proceedings and Property Act 1970, ss 1, 2, 26 (pp 2345, 2359), replacing Matrimonial Causes Act 1965, ss 15, 16(3), 20(1), 30 (pp 2230, 2231, 2232, 2240), replacing Matrimonial Causes Act 1950, ss 19(4), 20(3), 27 (pp 2128, 2129, 2131).

For Supreme Court of Judicature (Consolidation) Act 1925, s 190 (repealed), see p 2060.

(3)   In subsection (1) of the said section one hundred and ninety-one there shall be inserted after the word 'adultery' the words 'desertion, or cruelty.'

Note. For Supreme Court of Judicature (Consolidation) Act 1925, s 191(1) (repealed), see p 2061.

See now Matrimonial Causes Act 1973, s 24 (p 2487), replacing Matrimonial Proceedings and Property Act 1970, s 4 (p 2346), replacing Matrimonial Causes Act 1965, ss 17(2), 20(2) (pp 2231, 2232), replacing Matrimonial Causes Act 1950, s 24(1) (p 2130).

(4)   The following subsection shall be added to section one hundred and ninety-three of the principal Act:

  '(3)   The court may, if it thinks fit, on any decree of divorce or nullity of marriage, order the husband, or (in the case of a petition for divorce by a wife on the ground of her husband's insanity) order the wife, to secure for the benefit of the children such gross sum of money or annual sum of money as the court may deem reasonable, and the court may for that purpose order that it shall be referred to one of the conveyancing counsel of the court to settle and approve a proper deed or instrument to be executed by all necessary parties:

  Provided that the term for which any sum of money is secured for the benefit of a child shall not extend beyond the date when the child will attain twenty-one years of age.'

Note. Repealed by Matrimonial Causes Act 1950, s 34(1), Schedule, re-enacted by ibid, s 26(2), (3) (p 2131). See now Matrimonial Causes Act 1973, s 23 (p 2484), replacing Matrimonial Proceedings and Property Act 1970, s 3 (p 2346), replacing Matrimonial Causes Act 1965, s 34(3) (p 2242), replacing Matrimonial Causes Act 1950, s 26(3) (p 2131).

(5)   Section three of the Supreme Court of Judicature (Amendment) Act 1935 shall cease to have effect.

Note. Repealed by Matrimonial Causes Act 1950, s 34, Schedule.

11.   Extension of jurisdiction of courts of summary jurisdiction in matrimonial matters—*(1)   Among the grounds on which a married woman may apply to a court of summary jurisdiction under the Summary Jurisdiction (Married Women) Act 1895, for an order or orders under that Act there shall be included the ground that her husband has been guilty of adultery.*